THE EMANCIPATION OF WOMEN

THE EMANCIPATION OF WOMEN
An African Perspective

Florence Abena Dolphyne

Department of Linguistics
University of Ghana
Legon.

GHANA UNIVERSITIES PRESS
ACCRA
1991

Published by

Ghana Universities Press
P. O. Box 4219
Accra

ISBN: 9964 - 3 - 0188 - X

PRODUCED IN GHANA
Printed by Assemblies of God Literature Centre Limited,
Accra.

to
my daughter,
my nieces and
my nephews,
the younger members of the family,
who make such a difference to the African woman's home.

CONTENTS

Preface   ix

Chapter 1.   Traditional Practices   1

Marriage   1
Bride-wealth   7
Child marriage   11
Polygamy   14
Purdah   21
Widowhood   23
Inheritance of property   26
High fertility   30
Female circumcision   34

Chapter 2.   Promoting Women's Emancipation through
Specific Activities   41

Women in public life   45
Education   49
Income-generating activities   57
Agriculture   61
Food-processing   65
Handicrafts   80

Chapter 3.   The Way Forward   84

National Machineries and Non-Governmental
Organisations   86
International Agencies   92
Conclusion   101

References   103

Index   105

PREFACE

Ever since International Women's Year in 1975 highlighted the issue of the equality of men and women, women's issues, which previously were the concerns of voluntary women's societies, have attained national and international significance. During that year and throughout the ten years of the United Nations Decade for Women that followed, there were numerous research studies into the condition of women in different societies. There also were many conferences and seminars held at regional and international levels all over the world which afforded women the opportunity to identify, discuss and find ways of removing the obstacles that had been, and still were impeding women's emancipation and their full integration into the economic, social and political life of their various countries. From these research studies and discussions one thing became clear, that in spite of the differences in culture, in levels of education and in economic and industrial development of their countries, women the world over suffered similar types of injustice and discrimination within the family structure, in employment, in education and in access to professional training and so on. The difference between countries was one of degree, and as the evidence of discrimination built up, it became more and more obvious that, in order to achieve the objectives of the Decade, namely, Equality, Development and Peace, women, from developing as well as the industrialized countries, have to work together to fight the injustices that society has subjected them to for centuries.

It was in the spirit of women's solidarity therefore that many of the discussions of women's issues were conducted. The objective was to help women articulate their problems in clear terms and to work together in finding solutions to these problems.

It was disturbing for me, therefore, that at the Forum sessions (the meetings organized for representatives of Non-Governmental Organizations) of the Mid-Decade Conference held in Copenhagen, Denmark, in 1980, there was a clear polarization of positions held by women from the Western world in particular and women from Africa on certain burning issues about which both groups were obviously concerned, and for which both groups were equally anxious to find solutions. These issues related to certain traditional practices in African societies such as polygamy, bride-wealth (or bride price as it has been referred to by some anthropologists) and female circumcision. Both groups were equally of the opinion that these practices were an obstacle to the emancipation of women on the African continent. What they were not agreed on were the measures to be taken to eradicate them and the timing of such measures. The majority of the women from Western countries were for immediate legislation banning such practices. To them this was an obviously logical proposition: if all of us agree that these traditional practices are inimical to the welfare and total emancipation of women, then let the governments in those countries where these traditions persist legislate to make them illegal, and thereby set in motion the process that would put an end to them. This point of view was particularly strong at the sessions where female circumcision was discussed. At some of these sessions, gruesome details were given about the operation itself and the risks to the woman's health in later life, if she does not die from tetanus or some other form of infection after the circumcision.

The African women were put on the defensive. They tried to explain that these practices are deeply rooted in the traditions of the societies that practise them, and have religious and cultural significance in such societies. They pointed out that as educated African women, they realize that the principles underlying these practices are no longer tenable and they fully appreciate the need to work towards the total eradication of such practices. They have themselves been pressing for such eradication. However, what was needed most at this time, when most of the affected societies have a very high proportion of non-literate population living in rural areas, was education to make them aware of the health-hazards of female circumcision, for example, and improvement in their living conditions which will lower infant mortality - one major reason for frequent child-bearing in African women. Education and professional or vocational training were also needed to make young women economically independent and therefore make it unnecessary for a girl to be married off by her parents to a wealthy old man, who already has four wives, in order to ensure that she is well taken care of. They pointed out that many educated African women living in urban centres no longer practise these traditions, and it is clear that only sustained systematic education will achieve the results that everybody at the Conference was hoping for.

The educational programmes and the overall improvement in the living conditions of rural African societies that the African women participants at these discussions were asking for were too long-term for the Western women. They wanted to see immediate results, and the more radical among them felt the African women had let the side down, they had betrayed the women's cause.

While African women attending the Forum discussions were being accused of not being radical enough, their colleagues at the main Conference for government delegations were being accused of being too radical. They were not concentrating on what many of their Western counterparts considered to be "women's issues" - appropriate technology for women, organizing women's trade groups into viable co-operatives, and so on. Instead, they were dabbling in international political issues like racism in South Africa and the conflict in the Middle East, which, according to them, should be properly discussed at the United Nations General Assembly. Presumably, these are issues that should be properly discussed by men, since the delegations that go to the General Assembly are dominated by men.

The African women argued that all issues are women's

issues; that in any situation of deprivation, as was found in South Africa, or of war, as in the Middle East, or of poverty and hunger, as can be seen in a number of African countries, it is women and children who are the most vulnerable. For example, there is the Palestinian woman who has to bring up her children in the violent environment of a refugee camp, not knowing from one day to the next whether or not the camp would be raided, but fully conscious that she is raising her sons to be used as pawns in a conflict that seems to go on for ever. Then there is the South African woman who has to cope with bringing up her children single-handed in a squatter camp or in a remote settlement for blacks, miles away from her husband who works in a mine and who can only see his family for a short period once a year. There is also the woman in an African village who watches helplessly while her child dies of malnutrition and preventable diseases. For all these women, the issue of women's emancipation cannot be separated from the politics that brought about their particular situation. For all of them, the major problem is one of survival, and a necessary prerequisite for an improvement in their condition is that for the Palestinian woman, a satisfactory solution to the politics that created the war situation in the Middle East must be found. For the South African woman, the structures that suppress people on account of the colour of their skin in racist South Africa just have to be dismantled; and, for the woman in the developing African country, the inequities inherent in the present trade relations between indus-trialized countries and raw-material-producing Third World countries must be dealt with. In other words, the situation in which the former determine not only the price at which they sell their manufactured goods to developing countries, but also the price at which they buy raw materials from the developing countries, just has to change, because that is the main reason why African governments are unable to earn enough from their exports to provide basic education and adequate health facilities for all their citizens. By all means let us devise new appropriate technology to lighten the work-load of rural women, let there be programmes to educate women on primary health care, sanitation and such important matters; women should study the laws of their countries and agitate for the deletion or amendment of those laws that are discriminatory against women; and so the list of "women's concerns" continues. But it is also necessary for women to discuss, and to try to find solutions to international political issues that have far-reaching effects on the lives of women and their children in many countries

Since that Conference, I have become more and more conscious of the difference in approach to women's issues between Western women, especially 'feminists', and African women who are actively working for women's emancipation. I myself, as Vice-Chairman and later as Chairman of the National Council on Women and Development, the national machinery set up by the Ghana Government to ensure that the objectives of International Women's Year and the subsequent United Nations Decade for Women are achieved in Ghana, always knew that I was working for the total emancipation of women in Ghana. However, I never considered and still do not consider myself a 'feminist', for the term evokes for me the image of an aggressive woman who, in the same breath, speaks of a woman's right to education and professional training, her right to equal pay for work of equal value, her right to vote and to be voted for in elections at all levels, etc. as well as a woman's right to practise prostitution and lesbianism. It is this image of the feminist which made African men, some in highly-placed positions in government, and some women as well, rather uncomfortable about the idea of an international year for women. During 1975, it was usual for people to say that the whole idea of the equality of the sexes was foreign to Africa. Indeed, it was not until after the United Nations General Assembly had endorsed the Mexico International Women's Year Conference recommendation that 1976-1985 be declared the United Nations Decade for Women, that many countries in Africa began setting up offices like the Ghana National Council on Women and Development for ensuring that the objectives of the Decade were achieved in those countries. This is because it became clear from the details contained in the Mexico Programme of Action adopted at the 1975 International Women's Year Conference, that there was more at stake than the question of who cooked the dinner or changed the baby.

At the End-of-Decade Conference held in Nairobi, Kenya, in 1985, the rather hostile reception given the lesbian women's group attending the Forum again highlighted the fact that there are certain women's rights that are non-issues to African women. For most African women living in rural areas with no good drinking water, with no hospital or clinic within easy reach, no motorable roads to centres where certain essential services can be obtained, living in a drought-stricken area where there is a constant threat of famine and so on, the issue of women's rights is inextricably linked with that of survival. Their concerns relate to the provision of the basic necessities of life that will relieve them from the anxieties inherent in their existence, so that they can direct their energies towards making a worthwhile contribution to the achievement of a sustainable improvement in the conditions in which they live, and to the development of their society.

For most African women, therefore, the emancipation of women and the status of women in society are closely linked with national development, and during the Decade most of the activities initiated for women in Africa were women in development programmes.

What follows is an attempt, by someone closely associated with activities for women in Ghana during the Decade, to explain what she believes women's emancipation means to African women. This is based on her experience in Ghana and in a number of African countries, and from what she has gathered from women from different parts of Africa south of the Sahara.

This book is meant for those who are interested in issues that affect women, especially Third World women, whether these issues are related to age-old traditions that affect the status of women in society, or whether they are related to women-in-development programmes. Such programmes are included here because they are usually intended to ensure a more effective role for women in the development of their countries, thereby enhancing their own self-esteem as well as the recognition given them by the wider society.

I wish to express my sincere gratitude to Mrs. Grace Nartey for reading through an earlier version of this material, and for the very useful comments she made. My thanks also go to Mr. B.A.R. Braimah for the information on aspects of Moslem marriage.

To the Government of Ghana that gave me the opportunity to get involved in women's issues at the national and international levels by appointing me first as Vice-Chairman and later as Chairman of the Board of the National Council on Women and Development (NCWD), I wish to express my deep sense of gratitude.

I would also like to express my appreciation for the support and co-operation of my colleagues on the Board of the NCWD, the staff of the national and regional secretariats, and of the women of Ghana, without which much of the material in this book would not have been possible. Special mention must be made of Mrs. Justice Annie R. Jiagge, the first Chairman of the NCWD, for her pioneering work in making the NCWD an effective instrument for the promotion of women's emancipation in Ghana.

Finally, my husband, Kofi, and my daughter, Akuba, deserve special mention for patiently enduring my long absences from home during the eleven years that I served on the Board of the NCWD.

F. A D.

Chapter 1

TRADITIONAL PRACTICES

Every human society has a body of beliefs that regulate the way people behave and relate to each other in the society. Over the years, these beliefs and modes of behaviour are modified to suit the changing circumstances of the society concerned. African societies are no exception. What is different, however, is that as a result of the contact with Western civilization and the uneven influence that this civilization has had on African societies, one finds in every country a contrast between a very Westernized society usually comprising the educated people in the urban centres, and a traditional rural society whose beliefs and way of life often show that they have hardly been touched by Western culture.

In this chapter, we will consider some aspects of African culture which have a particular bearing on the issue of women's emancipation. These are customs, traditions and beliefs which have, over the years, helped to keep women under subjugation, and to make them feel generally inferior to men and incapable of operating at the same level as men in society. These are: the institution of marriage with its related issues of bride-wealth, child-marriage, polygamy, purdah, widowhood and inheritance of property, high fertility and puberty rites with specific reference to female circumcision.

Marriage

The institution of marriage is a very important one in all African societies. It is primarily a union between two families, rather than between two individuals. Traditionally, marriages are arranged between two families. When a young man decides he wants a particular woman for his wife, he tells his parents about it, and it then becomes the parents' responsibility and that of elders of the extended family to ask for the woman's hand from her parents. Before this is done, the parents try to find out all they can about the woman's family, whether there are any chronic or hereditary illnesses such as mental disorders in the family, whether there are any known criminals in the family, whether the women in the family are known to be respectful and hardworking or not, and so on. These are important matters that are known to ensure the stability or otherwise of a marriage. Emotional attachment between husband and wife was supposed to develop later, and therefore love between a young man and a young woman was not in itself considered legitimate grounds for marriage. If the young man's parents are not satisfied with what they find out, they will tell their son that he should look for someone else, or suggest somebody they approve of to him. In the same way, when a woman's family has been approached with a proposal of marriage from the man's parents, they also investigate the man's background and decide whether or not they would want their daughter to marry into that family.

It must be emphasized that the success of a marriage, even in modern times, depends to a considerable extent, on whether or not the two families are agreeable to the union, otherwise the several occasions, such as a child-naming ceremony, a wedding or a funeral, during which the two families will have to interact, may very well become a serious source of irritation and conflict that may result in the breakdown of the marriage. Even today, the educated urban young man and woman, who believe they are in love and would like to get married would do all they can to persuade their parents to agree to the union, that is if the parents are not happy about the relationship, rather than go to the marriage registrar's office to get married against their parents' wishes. A young man and a woman living in

2

Britain, Europe, America or anywhere else outside their own country, would not normally go through with a marriage ceremony until the man's parents have gone to ask for the woman's hand from her family. There are cases of Ghanaian young couples who meet while studying in Britain or America and get married without their parents' formal consent. However, before they return home to Ghana, or, as sometimes happens, soon after returning home, the man asks his relations to go to the woman's family to perform the necessary marriage custom so that the marriage would be recognized by the two families, and their children accepted by both families. If this is not done, and there is a funeral in, say, the woman's family, the man will be treated as an outsider and not as an in-law, and the same will apply to the woman if there is a funeral in the man's family. In this way, the society ensures that every marital union is properly a union between two families. This also means that normally divorce cannot be effected until members of both families have failed in their various attempts at reconciliation between husband and wife. Such attempts at reconciliation may even involve people outside the two families, such as respected elders in the community, especially, elders of religious bodies.

It must be mentioned, however, that in African societies, a man, his wife and his children do not constitute a family. The nuclear family as understood in Western societies is a new concept in African societies. Family, in the African sense, is the extended family. If it is a patrilineal society, where descent is traced through one's father, then it includes all the paternal relations - paternal uncles, aunts, cousins, nephews, nieces and so on. If it is a matrilineal society, where lineage is through the mother, then it includes all maternal relations.

Throughout Africa, there are three types of marriage that a man may opt for - marriage under Customary law, in which he can marry as many women as he feels he can support financially; Moslem marriage, in which a man can marry up to four women; and Ordinance marriage

3

(including Christian marriage) in which a man can only have one wife at a time. These reflect the three major cultures that have influenced African societies.

Moslem and Ordinance marriages have certain provisions which normally guarantee, to some extent, certain rights for a wife and children, and these are fairly uniform irrespective of the traditions and customs of the particular African society. The rights of a wife and children in Customary law marriages, on the other hand, are determined by the traditions of the particular African society. For example, in a patrilineal society, where lineage is traced through the father, the woman on marriage may become a member of her husband's extended family, and so are any children born in the marriage, as is the practice in many parts of eastern and southern Africa. However, in some patrilineal societies, such as those of the Ga and Dangme of Ghana, a woman is never a member of her husband's family, although her children are. In matrilineal societies, such as those found in parts of West Africa, a woman and her children never belong to the husband's family. Aspects of Customary law marriage such as the giving of bride-wealth, child-marriage, widowhood and the inheritance of property are discussed below. For the moment, it is sufficient to say that the majority of African women are married according to the traditions of their particular societies. Even those married under the Ordinance or Moslem law usually complete the procedures of Customary law marriage, sometimes referred to by such people as the 'engagement', before they go to the marriage registrar's office, or to the church to have the marriage registered and/or solemnized. This, in a sense, means that such couples have been married twice. In the Moslem system, the marriage ceremony may take place in the home in the presence of the Imam or any other person authorized to register a marriage.

Before I leave off the institution of marriage, let me mention something which, for the moment, is a non-issue for African women. This is the question of who does what in

4

the home. Every African woman grows up knowing that it is the woman who cooks the meals and generally sees to it that the house is clean and well-kept, and that everything is in its proper place. Whatever her level of education or professional status, she does not normally expect her husband to share the household chores with her. If the husband enjoys cooking and chooses to cook breakfast or dinner one day, she appreciates the fact that he is being helpful, but she does not expect him to do so as a matter of course. Husbands who, when they were living with their wives in Europe or America, willingly did the washing up or the laundry, put an end to that as soon as they return to Africa. The wives do not normally protest because they know their society does not expect a man to do such chores, and they will, therefore, not receive a sympathetic hearing even from their own relations, if they complained.

In general, most professional women employ house-helps to do the basic chores in the home. Very often, the salary of a house-help is the responsibility of the woman, for it is taken for granted that the person is there to do her job for her. And, not surprisingly, many professional women do not make a fuss about this, because they know the wider society is not yet ready to see any change in the present domestic arrangements. They cannot, therefore, expect sympathy or support for any move for such a change, especially when there are more important issues that affect the status and welfare of women.

It must be mentioned, though, that with urbanization and the need for a man and his wife to be working full-time in order to have a reasonable standard of living, one finds that husbands in lower-income homes, who cannot afford to engage the services of a house-help, are helping their wives with such chores as doing the laundry at the week-end or taking care of the children when the wife is cooking. Such people constitute only a small fraction of the population, but I mention it because it is an encouraging trend, even though it is bound to remain a limited urban phenomenon for many years. One may also mention the fact that even among

5

traditional rural farming communities, such as those of the Asante of Ghana, when a man and his wife move out of the village to live alone on their farm during the planting or harvest season, the man often assists the wife with some of the household chores, although this stops as soon as they move back into the bigger village community. This situation is very similar to that described above in relation to the African husband in Europe or America whose attitude to housework changes as soon as he returns home to Africa. It would appear, therefore, that the attitude of at least some African men to helping their wives at home is primarily dictated by the fear of their being ridiculed by the wider society as being dominated by their wives, an attitude that will take a long time to change.

Another marriage-related issue that may be mentioned here is that of the legitimacy of children born outside marriage. It has been stated above that a man may opt for one of three types of marriage. Customary law and Moslem marriage are potentially polygamous, while Ordinance (including Christian) marriage is monogamous. If a man opts for monogamy, he cannot have another wife while the marriage persists. However, any children that he has outside wedlock are considered legitimate, for in African societies legitimacy is determined by paternity. An 'illegitimate' child is one whose putative father refused to accept responsibility for the pregnancy that brought him into the world. In general, however, because a child is born into an extended family, the fact that he does not have a father does not normally create for him the complex problems that his counterpart in the Western world, for example, has to grapple with. This is because there is nothing in African societies like the stigma that goes with illegitimacy in Western societies.

The question of illegitimacy is one which, in recent years, is being discussed in some African countries, where women married in a monogamous system feel that children born outside wedlock should not be accorded the same rights as those born within it. Opponents of this view argue that the

6

concept of illegitimacy is foreign to African culture, and that it should not be introduced into our legal system, especially since it is known that, in some cultures, the stigma of illegitimacy has very serious adverse effects on children so regarded. In Ghana, the Law on Intestate Succession, passed in 1985, confirms the traditional view on legitimacy of children and stipulates that all children that a man has, inside and outside wedlock, have equal interest in his property.

Bride-wealth

Before a marriage is effected, gifts are normally exchanged between the families of the bride and the groom. However, what is provided by the groom is always substantially higher in value than what is provided by the bride, which, in some societies like the Ga or Akan of Ghana, consists of a meal that is shared by both families. In some southern African societies such as the Swazi of Swaziland, the bride gives expensive colourful blankets for selected in-laws. In the predominantly traditional non-literate society, the exchange of gifts is meant to be evidence of a contract of marriage between the two families.

In all African societies, it appears that what is given by the man, or in some cases demanded from him, as bride-wealth is determined by various factors. One of these is the status of the woman's family in the particular community, for example, whether or not she comes from a royal family or a family of wealthy and influential men and women. Another is the status of the woman herself, for example, whether or not she has had any formal education, and if she has, what level of education she has attained. Another important factor in determining the value of the bride-wealth appears to be whether the society concerned is matrilineal or patrilineal.

African societies can be broadly divided into two major types, matrilineal, where lineage is traced through the mother, and children born in a marriage belong to the mother's family; or patrilineal, where lineage is through the father and the children belong to the father's family. The bride-wealth given by a prospective husband to his would-be bride is generally much higher in patrilineal societies. This is because it is considered that the woman's family is going to lose her services, for example, on the farm, and she is also going to have children for the man's family to ensure its continuity, so in a sense, the man has to compensate her family adequately for these services that she would be performing for him. This is particularly true of the cattle-rearing societies of southern and eastern Africa, where a woman becomes part of a man's family on marriage. In these societies, a man may give anything between twenty and sixty cows for a wife. In some of these societies, such as among the Swazi, where the man cannot provide the total herd of cattle required as bride-wealth at the time of the marriage, an arrangement can be made for him to provide them in instalments. If he is unable to provide all of it before his death, his son will have to do that for him; otherwise, it will be a source of disgrace for both the man and the woman.

Women in such marriages have very little power. If they are ill-treated, they cannot normally ask for divorce because their parents will have to give back to the man the total herd of cattle that he gave as bride-wealth, and invariably the family would not be in a position to do so. The amount of ill-treatment that some of the women in such marriages put up with can be quite severe. Since they usually have no property of their own, and they cannot expect any protection or support from members of their own family, they suffer in silence, or, as sometimes happens, commit suicide. It must be mentioned, however, that in those patrilineal societies, such as the Ga and Dangme of Ghana, where the woman does not become a member of her husband's family, the bride-wealth given is not very substantial, and the women in these societies have greater freedom when it comes to divorce.

8

In the matrilineal society, a woman never becomes a member of her husband's family. She remains a member of her own family and so do the children that she bears. This means that what her own family loses on her getting married are her services on the farm, for example, but in the place of this, it is understood by her family that the husband is going to help her have children who will ensure the continuity of her own lineage. This is a greater advantage to her own family, so what is given as bride-wealth is relatively small. As with marriage in a patrilineal society, the bride-wealth has to be returned on divorce, and since it is usually not substantial, this can be readily done, so that marriage in a matrilineal society is, on the whole, less stable than marriage in a patrilineal one, but it also means that a woman in such a society is less likely to put up with ill-treatment from her husband. This is because she continues to enjoy the protection of members of her own family and may even continue to live in her family house after marriage. The confidence that such a woman has is reflected in the Akan (Ghana) saying which translates as "If you divorce me I will not eat stones".

Women from different parts of Africa generally agree that the bride-wealth that is demanded by a woman's relations, or what the would-be husband feels he should give as bride-wealth befitting his status and that of his would-be bride, is often too exorbitant. Many of them would want to see some restriction on the total value of the bride-wealth, whether in cattle, in gifts or in cash, for with the introduction of a cash economy into African societies, parents, especially those in urban centres, often ask for the cash equivalent of the bride-wealth, and this can be very high indeed. However, many women do not want to see an end to the practice because they feel that it is a source of disgrace for a woman to enter marriage without some bride-wealth being given to her and her relations. She will be ridiculed by the society as not being of much value in the eyes of her family. In the long run, it is the man, who has been saved the expenditure, who will at a later date turn round and insult

9

her as having been given away for free by her relations because they felt she was either a burden or not of much value to her family. It has already been explained that the bride-wealth, especially in the cattle-rearing patrilineal societies, is basically a compensation to the woman's family for the loss of her services. If no bride-wealth is given it would be a denial of a woman's worth to her husband in terms of the services she is expected to give, and the woman could be held up for ridicule.

It would appear, therefore, that this is one tradition that will not be abolished in the foreseeable future. Indeed, if there was legislation abolishing it, it would be impossible to enforce it, especially in the rural areas where people have very strong attachment to tradition. It may be possible, however, to appeal to traditional rulers and heads of religious bodies to use their influence to stipulate what the bride-wealth should consist of, so that an upper limit can be set. In appealing to such leaders in the society, the argument should not be that the bride-wealth system is a form of slavery because the high value of some bride-wealth seems to imply that the woman has been bought. Such an argument would be considered foreign to African thinking and western-inspired. What is more likely to receive sympathetic hearing is the argument that it is not healthy for a couple to start off married life with a debt on their hands, since very often people have to borrow money in order to obtain the appropriate type of bride-wealth, or give the cash equivalent of what is considered adequate and proper.

In Ghana, some congregations of the Presbyterian Church insist that if the bride-wealth given is more than a certain value, the church would refuse to bless the marriage. In order to ensure that this is enforced, an elder of the church is usually present at the customary marriage ceremony. This is one way of ensuring that the bride-wealth is kept within reasonable limits, and so far it seems to be achieving its objective in spite of the protests that some families sometimes make at these ceremonies. Chiefs and Traditional Councils in some parts of the country have also stipulated what the bride-wealth should consist of, and efforts are made to ensure that the rules are kept. It should be possible for women's organizations to put pressure on the leaders of their communities, especially traditional rulers, to work out a way of cutting down the cost of marriage so that ultimately it will become clear to every man in the society that the paltry amount that he spends in acquiring a wife cannot in any sense be construed to mean that he has 'bought' her. Such a move will meet with a great deal of resistance, especially in some of the cattle-rearing patrilineal societies where parents look to the marriage of their daughters as a sure means of acquiring property. It would appear, therefore, that a permanent solution to some of the family-related problems will have to be an overall improvement in the living standards of people. This will reduce parents' dependence on their children as their only insurance against poverty in their old age.

Child Marriage

As has been explained in the introduction to the discussion on marriage, arranged marriages are a feature of traditional African societies, and it is within this context that the following discussion on child marriage must be understood.

In some societies, an older man may indicate to the parents of a young girl that either he himself would like to marry the girl when she becomes of age or he would like to marry her for his son. This usually happens when there are very cordial relations between the two families or when the man believes the girl's family is known to have hard-working, well-behaved women.

If the girl's parents are agreeable, the man usually assumes financial responsibility for her upkeep, giving her clothing and other gifts, and paying for her education where applicable. In some cases, the young girl may be given to her prospective mother-in-law to bring up, so that she would

11

grow up knowing how things are done in her future husband's family. This also ensures that she becomes acquainted with her future in-laws long before she starts married life, and this helps to eliminate the trauma that she would otherwise experience if she had to leave her own parents' home at about age twelve or thirteen to start married life in her husband's home.

After the young girl reaches the age of puberty, the man decides when she is old enough to be taken to his house to start married life, and it is at such time that the formal marriage procedures are gone into, although very often the expenditure on her during childhood is taken into account in determining the value of the bride-wealth. If the girl is in school, she is invariably withdrawn from school when the man decides she is ready for marriage, and so such girls very often do not complete formal education. In many cases, this is a way of ensuring that the girl does not become too sophisticated and have ideas about falling in love with somebody else.

Although such arrangements may have worked in the past, it often happens in modern times that a girl may refuse to marry the man she had been promised to when she was a child. This creates problems for everybody. If the parents are unable to persuade her into marrying the man, they have to refund to him all the money that he had spent on her since he made the proposal of marriage. This is often impossible for them to do, for if they were rich, they probably would not have allowed the future husband to spend that much money on her in the first place. In some societies, as in parts of northern Ghana, a girl may get out of this difficult situation by 'eloping' with her lover, but the lover will have to refund to the rejected man all the money that he had spent on her, which he may not be in a position to do. Invariably, what happens is that the girl is forced to go and live with her husband, sometimes with very unpleasant consequences, for she may be locked up for some time, or otherwise coerced into agreeing to stay in the husband's home and live as a married woman. Since such girls cannot expect any protection from their parents, they either submit to their new way of life or, as sometimes happens if they have the guts, they may run away to an urban centre where they can hopefully get 'lost'. It is known that quite often such girls end up as prostitutes in the urban centres for they very often have no skills that will get them a job, and they usually avoid people they know, who can help them, for fear of being sent back to their angry husbands or parents.

The experiences that these young brides - sometimes as young as twelve years - often go through are quite traumatic. Because of their young age and because their bodies are not sufficiently fully developed to cope with child-bearing, they sometimes suffer permanent damage to their health at the birth of their first child.

Most African countries have incorporated into their Constitutions the provisions of the Universal Declaration of Human Rights. Many have signed, and some have even ratified, the United Nations Convention on the Elimination of All Forms of Discrimination Against Women which, among other things, requires member states to "ensure, on a basis of equality of men and women:

> the same right freely to choose a spouse and to enter
> into marriage only with their free and full consent."
> (Article 16, 1(b).)

However, one is yet to see in any of these countries, a law banning child-marriage. Those who support the practice say that it is the way society ensures the moral uprightness of its women, who, as mothers of the next generation, must have the highest moral standards so as to be able to impart the same to their children. They must, therefore, be married off early to ensure that they do not become wayward. But as has been pointed out, the same practice has forced some girls to run away from home and end up as prostitutes. Some men also claim it is a source of rejuvenation for adult men, although there is no medical evidence to support this claim.

In the societies where the practice persists, it is usually

the men who support it, and unfortunately they are the law-makers and the traditional rulers, and they cannot be expected to legislate against it. One possible way of dealing with the problem is for there to be legislation stipulating a minimum age for marriage. But perhaps a more effective way of eradicating the practice is for governments in the various countries to pass and enforce a law making formal education compulsory for all children, and stipulating a minimum number of years - at least 9 years - during which children should stay in school. This would at least ensure that until they complete compulsory formal education at about age 14 or 15, girls would not be forced to go and start married life, even though they may have been promised in marriage at an earlier age, for the practice of arranged marriages is one that will be difficult to eliminate completely, since it will be impossible to enforce or monitor its elimination.

Again, one comes back to the question of the economic prosperity of African countries. In the absence of such economic prosperity, it will be impossible for any government to provide free primary school education for all children, and without such free education, no government can insist or ensure that parents send all their children to school, and keep them there for the stipulated minimum period.

Polygamy

An Asante (Ghana) folktale that provides a rationale for polygamy goes like this: A man who had been married for about two years decided to take on a second wife. His wife thought there was no need for that since she felt they were getting on perfectly happily. She already had one child, and was likely to have more. The man argued that she alone could not provide for him all the things he needed at the times he needed them, but the woman insisted he had no basis for that claim. To prove his point, the man one day said

14

he wanted to eat Asante kenkey, a preparation from corn-dough, and the woman had that day to prepare it for him. The woman accepted the challenge and started by beating the maize in a very deep mortar to remove the skin from the maize, for the kenkey is made from polished maize. After removing the skin, she pounded the maize in another mortar to break it up. She then ground it on a big grinding stone to get a smooth paste, for this was the age when there were no cornmills. By this time she was not only physically exhausted, but both palms were in blisters, and she had difficulty mixing the corn-dough to the right consistency for making the kenkey. She eventually gave up, went to the elders of her family and asked them to go and apologize to the man on her behalf for being so stubborn, and to tell him that she was perfectly agreeable to his marrying a second wife. And that, according to the story, is how men started marrying more than one wife.

This story illustrates how society conditions its members into accepting the norms of the society. A young girl in a village would hear this story told over and over again, and by the time she is of age she would know that it is not possible for one woman to satisfy the needs of her husband, and therefore she should be prepared to share her husband with co-wives. It is for this reason that while the more radical feminists would want to see legislation banning the traditional practices that are seen to be demeaning to a woman's status in society, it is clear to most African women fighting for women's emancipation that such legislation will at best affect only a fraction of the educated women living in urban communities. The rest of the population will continue to practise them until the inimical effects of the particular traditional practice have been demonstrated to them in no uncertain terms, or until, as suggested above in the case of child-marriage, something new and seen to be beneficial, such as formal education, has been put in its place.

In traditional African societies, men have usually married more than one woman in order to have more hands to help them work on their farms. More wives meant more children, and the larger a man's farm, the more wives and children he had. Thus, over the years, the number of wives a man had was seen as a reflection of his affluence. In recent years, formal education has meant a reduction in the labour provided by children, and hired labour has also meant a reduction in the value of the labour provided by wives, although they became useful supervisors of the hired labour. In modern times, therefore, the usefulness of wives as free labour has been considerably reduced, but the practice of polygamy still persists.

One of the main reasons for this state of affairs is that all African societies believe that a woman must be married, and marriage confers on a woman a high degree of respectability in her community. And so whatever her level of education, professional status or economic independence, an African woman would not normally choose to remain single, although it is also true to say that higher education and professional status do confer a very high degree of respectability on a woman, irrespective of her marital status. One must add that marriage also confers respectability on a man. An unmarried man is normally regarded as irresponsible: he cannot even assume responsibility for a wife and children. A woman is also expected to have children to prove her womanhood, and it is true to say that the respect and status that motherhood confers on a woman is greater than that conferred by marriage per se. A young woman who has children outside marriage is generally regarded as a disgrace to herself and to her family, and so to have children, a woman must be married, and it does not matter how many wives the man already has. For these reasons, one finds that some of the strongest opponents to any legislation banning polygamy are women, even highly educated women.

There are other reasons why many women find polygamy a convenient arrangement. There are women who have been able to continue their education and have professional training after marriage and the birth of one or

16

two children because as the third or fourth wife, they found willing and competent mothers for their children in the senior co-wives. Understandably, this can only happen if the junior wife gives them due respect, and there is harmony in the home.

The freedom of movement that a polygamous marriage makes possible for women can also be seen in the activities of market women. In, especially, the non-Moslem parts of West Africa, retail trade in agricultural produce and in manufactured goods is dominated by women. They have full control over the money they earn, and many of them have, without the help of husbands, brothers or other male relation, been able to give their children education and professional training. Many of these women are married in a polygamous system, and they find it a very convenient arrangement, for a woman can travel for days buying goods from one part of the country and transporting them to the market centres without having to worry about a husband whose meals have to be ready at specific times. There will be another wife to take care of that while she is away. Of course, it also can happen that if the man is not too well organized, and has not made proper arrangements, he may go hungry because each wife expects one or the other co-wife to be cooking for him. This situation is summed up in an Asante (Ghana) proverb which translates as "It is hunger that killed the man with many wives", a statement which implies that although traditional society approves of polygamy, it also feels that a man can have a wife too many.

Some educated women, especially those of the Moslem faith, whose religion does not give any protection against polygamy because it allows a man up to four wives, will tell you that they would not mind being the second, third or fourth wife. Their reason is that they will have time to concentrate on their profession when it is not their turn to keep house for the husband. The cynics among them will add that while monogamy does not guarantee a husband's fidelity, in a polygamous marriage, a woman at least has some idea of where her husband is likely to be when he is not with her.

17

Some women who support polygamy have even argued that it is justified on account of the ratio of women to men in their countries, although one is yet to find an African country whose census figures show that women are around 65 per cent of the population, which will be a basis for at least some of the men being entitled to no more than two women each. The fact is that since most women do not have any formal education, and since they do not need to undergo any formal vocational training, having learnt whatever trade their mothers are engaged in from observation and participation, there are, at any given time, more girls who are ready for marriage than there are marriageable men. The young men of their age or a little older will still be in school or will be struggling to acquire some property, such as their own farm, which will enable them to pay for the bride-wealth required, and also make them capable of maintaining a wife and children. Girls, therefore, marry men who are often many years older than they are, and it is not unusual to find a woman in traditional society addressing her husband as 'Master' or by some other title that duly reflects his superior position. She never calls him by his name.

For the present, most African women, especially the rural majority, believe that polygamy as practised in African societies, is to be preferred to the situation one finds in Western societies where, in the strict monogamous system, a man may be married to one woman but keeps one or more mistresses. This is what is happening in many 'monogamous' marriages among educated Africans. There is also the modern trend of successive polygamy where a man in his life-time may be married to several women, only he divorces one before he marries the next - a system that creates problems for children born in each succeeding marriage. The polygamous system in traditional African societies at least gives equal status to co-wives, although usually the most senior commands respect and the newest wife is the favoured one.

One should not, however, underrate the emotional strain that individual women go through in polygamous marriages, especially in modern times. In the past, a woman married for economic security, and she would put up with infidelity and with other forms of cruelty on the part of her husband as long as he provided for her and her children. Now that women are becoming economically independent, they have other expectations in marriage, the major ones being affection and companionship. This is particularly true of educated women. When these expectations are not fulfilled because a husband is seriously involved in extra-marital relations, some women decide to break off the marriage, especially if they can, on their own, take full responsibility for the upbringing of their children. This has led to the creation of the impression that education, especially higher education, for women is responsible for the increase in divorce rate. Men and women of the older generation, in particular, cannot appreciate the feeling of betrayal that a woman, who has had a happy marriage with her husband and shared confidences with him for many years, has when her husband decides to take on another wife, or when he starts having children outside his officially monogamous marriage. A woman who decides to divorce her husband because he has a serious relationship with another woman is, therefore, considered to be over-reacting, and she cannot normally expect much sympathy from either friends or relations, especially if there are children in the marriage. She will be told that divorce is bad for the children. Older women in her family will tell her about several instances in which a woman had patiently tolerated her husband's infidelity, and then several years later he had come back to her, having realized the uselessness of those other relationships. In other words, if the woman waits long enough, she will have her husband back, and the marriage will be as good as new. Of course, they never tell of those cases where the women have stayed on and suffered in silence, ending up growing old prematurely, losing their interest in life and, sometimes, even losing their minds. They do not also tell of the rivalries that can and do develop between brothers and sisters from different mothers, not to

19

mention the rivalries between co-wives and the effect they have on their children.

It is quite clear that African societies are, in general, not yet ready to consider polygamy, or monogamy with extramarital relations, as a major issue. This is why educated African women working for women's emancipation do not treat it as a priority, for they feel the time is not yet right for serious discussion on the issue. Moreover, the effect, on women, of polygamy and extra-marital relations on the part of husbands is still a very private issue, and when one considers the obvious and demonstrable inimical effects that practices like child-marriage, bride-wealth and circumcision have on women, it is difficult to accord polygamy the same priority status among pressing issues that affect women in Africa.

In recent years, many men, especially those in the urban centres, have become keenly conscious of the need to educate and provide a fairly high standard of living for their children. This, coupled with the economic hardships that almost all African countries are experiencing, have made many men come to the realization that it is difficult enough for them to cope with a small family, and they would not even contemplate acquiring a second wife who will insist on having her quota of children, at least three or four, much less a third and a fourth.

It would appear, therefore, that the desire for a better standard of living for one's family, and the economic constraints of modern life are the two major factors that will eventually make men see the undesirability of marrying more than one woman at a time. It may be mentioned here that the Christian religion, with its insistence on monogamy, has helped to reduce the incidence of polygamy to some extent. Moreover, some men, who grew up in polygamous homes and suffered from the rivalries that existed between co-wives and between their children, no longer consider marriage to more than one woman a worthwhile venture.

One practical way of reducing the incidence of polygamy is to encourage professional and vocational training for girls, so that they marry at a later age when it is possible for them to find husbands among their own age group. Such professional training will also mean that a woman will be reasonably economically independent, so that it would not be necessary for her to become a second or a third wife to a man simply because he is well-to-do and therefore able to provide for her. In other words, the need for economic security will no longer be a motive for a girl to get into marriage, whether polygamous or not.

Purdah

"We Hausa women do not dirty our hands, we do not work in the fields." This is what a Moslem Hausa woman in Kano, northern Nigeria, told me.

Purdah is a tradition, apparently a Persian tradition that has found its way into Islam, which requires that a woman, on marriage, should not be seen by any man other than her husband. She, therefore, has to stay indoors during the day, going out only in the evenings when she can sit outside and have a chat with her friends or visit her relations. If she must go out during the day, her face must be properly veiled from prying eyes. Normally, purdah is observed for a few weeks after marriage, to give the new couple time to be together and to get to know each other, since there usually is no period of courtship before marriage.

In some societies, however, if the man is rich, he can afford to keep his wives in purdah for as long as he likes, sometimes until they are fairly old when, presumably, they are no longer attractive to other men. In the very strict Moslem society of Kano, some married women, like the one I met, stay in purdah for the better part of their lives.

The Kano Hausa woman was the most senior of four wives. Each of them had her own room in the husband's two-storey house, and they took turns to cook for the household. At 35, her 22-year old daughter already had a 7-year old son. The woman never had any formal education, but her daughter had eight years of primary school before, at 14, she was married to a 28-year old engineer. At the time I visited her home, it was the turn of the second wife to cook for the family, and the other three women had very little to do. The youngest wife had had some formal education, and had grown up in an urban setting in the southern part of Nigeria, where women have more freedom of movement, and it was obvious she could not cope with having to stay indoors most of the day. We stopped at her door for a brief chat, and I noticed, to my utter surprise and disbelief, and to the embarrassment of the most senior wife, that she was smoking. Later, the first wife remarked with obvious disapproval, "These girls from the south are impossible. She smokes all day." I did not ask how the husband felt about her smoking.

To go back to the woman's earlier statement, I almost envied her the pride with which she spoke about her not having to work. And who wouldn't want to be a lady of leisure, not having to rush out to work in the morning with barely enough time for a quick breakfast; not having to spend half of the working day putting up with unreasonable customers, difficult school children or bad-tempered bosses; not having to rush back home after work to fix dinner for a hungry husband, and at the same time try to present a calm outside for children demanding the love and attention of a mother they have missed for a whole day? Who wouldn't envy the Kano Hausa woman who does not have to dirty her hands with work?

But then there was the youngest wife whose only escape from the boredom of her existence was to chain-smoke. She was 18 when she was married off by her parents to her rich husband. The freedom she had enjoyed as a child growing up in an urban setting in southern Nigeria had not prepared her for her new way of life, and she was obviously living under a great deal of stress.

The practice of purdah is obviously another example of the inequality that exists between men and women in some African Moslem societies. But more than its being another

22

instance of how society ensures male superiority, it is a clear waste of human resources - a waste of 'woman-power' as an essential part of the manpower resources available to a country. It is from this point of view that any attack on the system must be made, and any move for a change must be initiated by members of the Moslem community, if it is to have any chance of success. Most Moslem societies do not keep women in purdah for the best part of their lives, and in such societies there is evidence of the value of working women's contribution to improvement in the condition of life of their families, as well as to the development of their countries. It should be possible to gather such evidence and to use it to persuade Moslem leaders to steadily reduce the period of purdah until the practice is ultimately abolished.

Widowhood

When a man dies it is because his wife is an unlucky woman whose ill-luck has caused her husband's death. In some communities in Ghana, it is this belief that underlies the treatment that a woman goes through at the death of her husband. In these communities, there is a strong belief that such a woman is likely to bury a second and a third husband, after which the fourth, if she can find one, will survive her. She must, therefore, purge herself of the ill-luck that is dogging her. The period for such purging varies from one society to another, but what runs through most of the widowhood rites is that the woman must be put through a certain amount of discomfort. If she is not liked by her in-laws, the sisters-in-law in particular make it their business to generally make life unpleasant for her, especially if they believe their brother had been extremely good to her and, as a result, had neglected them. She is not normally supposed to sleep in a bed till after the fortieth day of the death of her husband, and so she sleeps on a mat on the floor. During the first forty days, the widow is confined to the house, usually that of the husband's family, unless special permission is given for her to continue with the widowhood rites in her own house. She cannot engage in any economic activity for a considerable length of time, and she may have to wait for six months or even a year before going about her normal business, especially if she is self-employed.

On the first anniversary of the husband's death, the widow discards her mourning clothes and starts normal life again. In some communities, there is an end-of-widowhood ceremony at this time, involving the slaughtering of a sheep and feasting. A widow in such a community cannot discard her mourning clothes until she has performed this ceremony. If she cannot afford a sheep, drinks and the other things needed for the ceremony on the anniversary of her husband's death, she continues in mourning clothes until she is able to do so.

The practice of widowhood rites is again one of the traditional practices that clearly shows the inequality between the sexes. A man is never responsible for his wife's death unless there is very clear evidence that she died as a result of physical violence on her by the husband. Even in such a situation, the woman may be blamed for being difficult and insubordinate, thus forcing the husband to be violent towards her. A widower must also undergo certain rites to rid himself of the ill-luck and the contamination that death is generally considered to bring. But these are done with the minimum of discomfort, the worst being confinement to the house for about a week or two.

In Ghana, after considerable debate, a law was eventually passed banning widowhood rites. However, women who had been pressing for such a law realized, to their dismay, that so strong is the belief that a widow may be haunted by the ghost of her husband if she does not perform these rites, that there are widows who are still willing to go through with them, in spite of the law. Some widows also feel that if they refuse to perform these rites, it will be an insult to the memory of the husband who, in his lifetime, had been so good to them. Of course, the law ensures that widows who do not wish to perform the rites are protected. But what is

24

abundantly clear is that while such progressive laws reflect the society's desire to break away from undesirable aspects of its culture, they are only effective to the extent that the wider society is prepared to conform to the provisions contained in them. In the case of the widowhood rites, enforcement of the law banning them depends primarily on the willingness of the women whom the law seeks to protect to be so protected. This means that while laws aimed at the eradication of certain traditional practices may be desirable and necessary, what is more important is a systematic programme of education to make the society as a whole, and the women in particular, appreciate the need for a change in attitude to those traditional practices.

While on widowhood, one may mention the practice in many African societies where the successor to the dead man may inherit his widow(s) as well. In some of these societies, the widow has the right to choose a husband from among the dead husband's brothers. The widow may also refuse to re-marry into her husband's family, although in such a situation, her family, in most cases, will have to return the bride-wealth that was given at her marriage. Returning the bride-wealth indicates that the marriage between her family and her dead husband's is broken, and that she is free to re-marry.

A typical feminist reaction to a widow being married by the dead husband's relation is that it makes a woman part of a man's estate that may be disposed of or inherited at his death. However, given the fact that the women in many of these societies have no independent source of livelihood, such re-marriage into the husband's family guarantees that she and her children will be taken care of. The only way to put an end to such a practice is, as suggested under polygamy, to give women skills that will make them economically independent, so that marriage will not be the only avenue open to them in their search for economic security.

Inheritance of Property

It has already been pointed out that most marriages in Africa are polygamous, which means that a man's property has to be shared among his many widows and children on his death. If a man dies intestate, that is, without leaving a will indicating how the property must be shared, this creates a problem because of the variety of claims that the different wives and children may have on specific items of the property. Moslem law stipulates how a man's property may be shared after his death and therefore the problem, to some extent, is not very great where the marriage is a Moslem one. The same is true, to some extent, of Ordinance and Christian marriage. There is a major problem, however, when a man dies intestate in a polygamous Customary law marriage. Even in an officially monogamous Christian or Ordinance marriage, the common practice of men having children outside their monogamous marriage creates problems over the sharing of property when the man dies intestate.

It has also been stated that African societies are either matrilineal, where lineage is traced through the mother, or patrilineal, where lineage is traced through the father. In a matrilineal society, children do not have an automatic right to their father's property, but they can inherit the property of their maternal uncle. A situation, therefore, arises where a woman and her children may be thrown out of the matrimonial home on the death of her husband, and the house inherited by the husband's nephews, that is, his sister's children. The problem is further compounded when a woman from a patrilineal society marries a man from a matrilineal society, for, while her children cannot inherit their father's property, because he comes from a matrilineal society, where it is his sister's children who have a right to his property, they cannot inherit their maternal uncle's property either, because their mother comes from a patrilineal society.

The point has also been made that in a society where

26

most people do not have social security benefits, parents look to their children as their main insurance against poverty in their old age. When, therefore, a man is survived by a parent, the wife or wives and their children have to contend with the interest that the parent also has in the property.

All these factors have been a source of strain and worry for women, for in general, most people, both men and women, do not make wills until they are very old. The general feeling is that one makes a will when one is near death, certainly not at forty or fifty, when death seems so far away. Many men, therefore, die intestate, even highly educated men, and their deaths are often followed by interminable law suits to determine who is entitled to what.

In Ghana, the inheritance of property was identified as one of the major causes of instability in marriage, for wives have no interest in their husband's property whether the society is matrilineal or patrilineal. Many women would, therefore, not embark on joint ventures with their husbands for fear of losing everything, especially if the husband comes from a matrilineal society. She may also have to share the property either with co-wives or, if hers is a monogamous marriage, with children the wife may not have been aware of, who usually surface when the man dies. Many women who have the money will build a house of their own rather than help their husband build. They are also careful to let everyone, especially their in-laws, know the particular items of furniture or major household equipment that they had bought for the house so that no one is in doubt as to who owns what.

For years, a law on Intestate Succession was on the agenda of the Ghana Law Reform Commission. The law was discussed over and over again by all sectors of the society, and women's organizations, in particular, sent their comments and recommendations on the proposed law.

People from matrilineal societies, who are in the majority in the country, opposed the law because they felt that any law that made provision for children to inherit their father's property would be an imposition of the patrilineal system on the matrilineal one. This, they argued, would ultimately undermine the cultural basis of the matrilineal society. In Ghana, as stated earlier, wives traditionally have no interest in their husband's property in either the patrilineal or the matrilineal society. If a husband, in his lifetime, felt that his wife had been good to him, he made a formal gift of a house or a farm or some such valuable property to her, for which her family would formally thank him. Such property would remain hers after the death of her husband.

In 1985, as a major contribution to the efforts initiated during the UN Decade for Women to improve the lot of women in Ghana, the Ghana Government passed the Law on Intestate Succession, which makes provision for surviving spouse(s) and all the children that a man claimed to be his during his lifetime, to inherit the greater proportion of his self-acquired property. The law also makes some provision for surviving parent(s). Only a very small percentage of the property goes to the extended family. It must be pointed out that the law makes specific provision for the surviving spouse, so that a wife is provided for whether or not she had children in the marriage.

This is one area in which legislation has made a dramatic impact on a traditional practice that was oppressive to women. Now, a widow in Ghana does not have to worry about being ejected from her matrimonial home on the death of her husband. Hopefully, this provision will help foster stability in marriage, as well as mutual co-operation between husband and wife, at least within monogamous marriages.

The application of the Law on Intestate Succession to polygamous marriages is a little more complicated, not so much because all wives and their children have an equal interest in the man's property, but because the law gives equal rights to men and women in the inheritance of property. In other words, it makes it possible for the surviving spouse, a husband or a wife, to inherit the self-acquired property of the deceased. This means that a woman in a polygamous marriage, who wants to ensure that only her children, and not her husband and his wives as well, inherit her property, has to make a will to say so. A certain amount of education is going on to bring this home to women, especially the rich market women in the urban centres, many of whom have a lot of property.

In a number of African countries, the inheritance of property, where a man dies intestate, is done according to the type of marriage contracted. This means that it is done according to the Customary law of the particular society, if it was a Customary law marriage; according to Moslem law if it was a Moslem marriage; and according to Ordinance law if it was an Ordinance law or a Christian marriage. The absence of a uniform law on intestate succession in these countries means that many women, especially those married under Customary law, are at the mercy of their in-laws on the death of their husbands. This should not be so, and something has to be done to relieve a widow of the anxiety and the feeling of insecurity that aggravates the deep sense of loss that she must feel at the death of her husband.

As has been pointed out, this is one area in which legislation can, in a very short time, make an impact on the plight of women. Women's organizations should work in close collaboration with women lawyers in their countries to bring pressure on their governments in order to ensure that there is legislation that gives equal rights to men and women in the inheritance of property. Such legislation will ensure that widows in the society can have a fair share of the property that they helped their husbands to acquire, irrespective of the type of marriage they contracted. In Ghana, the women lawyers association (FIDA, Ghana Chapter) has instituted legal aid to assist women who cannot afford the services of lawyers, including widows whose in-laws may try to deprive them and their children of their entitlements under the Intestate Succession Law.

High Fertility

Children are of special value to both men and women in African societies. It has been pointed out that the respect and status that motherhood confers on a woman is greater than that conferred by marriage per se. For this reason, and also in order to fulfil a personal desire for motherhood, sometimes even educated professional women, some of them brought up in strict Christian homes, will rather have children outside wedlock than remain childless. The point has also been made that a woman needs to have children to ensure the continuity of her own lineage in a matrilineal society, or that of her husband, in a patrilineal society. The more children she has, the better. There is often considerable pressure on a young woman to get married and start a family. Such pressure does not only come from mothers who are anxious to see their grandchildren in their lifetime, but also from well-meaning friends and relations who feel that delaying child-bearing for too long may result in childlessness. One may add that the love of children, not necessarily one's own, is a greatly-admired virtue in women, and a childless woman, whether married or single, is greatly admired and respected if she can nurture a mother/child relationship between herself and the nephews and nieces, and even the stepchildren that she brings up. The more such children she has the greater the respect accorded her by society. It is, therefore, considered unnatural in traditional society for a healthy woman, especially a healthy married woman in her late twenties or early thirties, who is capable of having children, to wilfully choose to limit the size of her family.

A man must also have children to ensure that the names of his forebears survive into the future, for it is the man who names a child. In order that his own name does not disappear, he must have sons who will name their children after him, and the more sons he has the better. If his wife gives birth to girls only, she will have to continue having more children until a son is born. More often than not, a

30

man will either marry other women who, hopefully, will bear him sons, or if he is married according to Ordinance law or Christian marriage, he may try to have a son outside his marriage. A woman may even be divorced for the simple reason that she has not been able to bear sons for her husband; so high is the premium placed on sons by men, who want to ensure that their names do not disappear. Very often, an educated couple who may have planned to have three children will end up with five, or six in their desire to have children of both sexes, for while sons are needed to ensure the survival of family names, daughters, who ensure the continuity of the lineage, are of special value in a matrilineal society. It must be pointed out that adoption is as yet not a very acceptable alternative to having one's own children.

The point has also been made that children are the only insurance that parents have against poverty in their old age, so the more children they have, the more likely they are to be taken good care of when they are no longer able to work. The high level of infant mortality, especially in rural communities, as a result of poor sanitation, poor nutrition, the prevalence of communicable diseases and the inadequacy of medical services, has meant that couples must have many children in order to ensure that some survive into adulthood. Mention must also be made of the high toll that sickle cell anaemia, a hereditary disease common among the black race, takes on the lives of children in Africa.

In the late 1960s and early 1970s when the world was suddenly awakened to the threat of a population explosion, Third World countries in particular became the target for internationally-funded programmes on family planning and population control. In Ghana, family-planning posters depicted the ideal happy family as one with three children. There were slogans on the radio encouraging people to have fewer children so that the government could provide enough schools for their education, and employment for school-leavers. The ineffectiveness of these slogans must have soon become clear, for they were taken off the air. People

31

usually have the number of children they believe the, can look after. Whether the government can or cannot provide for those children in later life is not a matter of immediate concern.

In another African country, the family-planning poster depicting the ideal family, was one with a smiling well-dressed couple and two happy children, a boy and a girl. In contrast to this was the picture of a couple with eight children, all of them in tattered clothes and looking miserable. The posters had a negative effect. Ordinary people thought of the couple with only two children as selfish, for they should have had more children to spread their wealth, and the happiness to be derived from it, to a few more children. The large family, though looking poor, evoked a more sympathetic reaction. People believe that it is always possible for one or two of many children to make it in the world and take care of the rest.

It should be obvious that for new or non-traditional ideas such as limiting family size to be accepted, especially by rural communities, and for new programmes at improving the quality of life of a people to be successful, it is essential that the cultural values of the particular society are taken into consideration in devising ways of putting the new ideas across. The shift in emphasis in family-planning programmes from family size to the spacing of births to protect the health of the mother and that of her child, is having a better impact, for the idea is not alien to African societies. Polygamy and, in some societies, taboos forbidding sex with a lactating mother, have been ways in which this has been ensured in traditional society. What is now needed in order to reduce high fertility among African women is for girls to marry at a much older age than they do at the moment, so as to reduce the child-bearing period. The only way this can be achieved is for girls to complete formal education and have vocational or professional training before marriage. Formal education for girls is in itself an effective tool for limiting family size, for it is quite clear that because educated women want to give their children a much higher standard of living than they themselves had as children, and also give them the best education available, they tend to have fewer children. Sex and family life education for, especially, teenage boys and girls is also needed to reduce the incidence of precocious pregnancies among school girls, and to ensure that the girls complete their formal education. In addition, women need to be assured that the few children that they bring into the world will survive into adulthood, by the provision of basic amenities such as good drinking water, immunization and medical services within easy reach. In the absence of these, family-planning programmes will continue to have very little or no impact on the large rural population. When everybody in a village has been witness to a woman losing three children to measles within two months, it will be difficult, if not impossible, to persuade any young woman in that village not to have more than three children. Advocating for two children only is certainly out of the question in such a situation. If much of the funding that goes into the provision of contraceptive devices were spent on the provision of good drinking water, facilities for immunization, and a general improvement in the living conditions of rural communities, much better results would be achieved. The harsh economic environment in which many people live in Africa today, and the desire of most parents to give their children some basic education, are important factors that have, in recent years, affected family size.

Another important factor is an improvement in the status of women. It is known that very often, a woman who is bogged down with frequent child-bearing, and even when this is aggravated by poverty, will continue to have more children because her husband wants her to. Some women in desperation have, on their own, gone to family-planning clinics without their husbands' consent. When this is discovered, it usually creates such tension in the home that the woman invariably gives up using the birth control device that she had been given at the clinic. Such women usually have no independent source of income, and have very little

33

or no say in the home, whether it has to do with the children's upbringing or with how many children she must have. Married women who are economically independent, and who can, therefore, contribute substantially to the family income, usually have a greater say in matters affecting the family, and they can, and indeed do have a say in how many children they want to have. The women in development programmes, such as those discussed in Chapter 2, have had the effect of improving women's income-earning capacity, and this has given them greater self-confidence as well as the respect of members of their community, and husbands have had to take note of what the women have to say about the number of children they want to have, for they contribute financially to the raising of those children. It would appear, therefore, that in addition to formal education, another effective way of reducing high fertility among African women is an improvement in their income-earning capacity. The promotion of income-generating projects for rural women in particular, should therefore be a priority in the national programmes on population control.

Finally, an improvement in the status of women will ultimately lower the incidence of polygamy, which, because of competition in child-bearing among co-wives, is a significant factor in the high fertility levels among African women.

Female Circumcision

An educated Kenyan woman from a society that practises female circumcision had this to say about her own experience: Her parents were both educated, and had decided that she would not be circumcised. When her friends in a girls' boarding school, where she had her secondary education, found out about this, she became an object of ridicule. On occasion, when they were all happily having a girlish chat, somebody would interrupt the conversation and say that she had not attained adulthood yet, and did not

34

qualify to be sharing their jokes. These occasions caused her a lot of pain and humiliation, but she managed to survive them. After formal education and professional training, she got married under Ordinance law, and had three children - two boys and a girl. The husband came from the same part of the country, and they had a happy married life until the husband started an affair with another woman, and decided to divorce her and marry the other woman. The husband had the full backing of his relations when they learnt that she was not circumcised, for that meant she was unclean, and they would not have their son, brother, etc. continue living with an unclean woman. So the marriage was dissolved. But the worst was yet to come. Theirs is a patrilineal society where children belong to their father's family whether the couple are divorced or not. The man and his relations decided that the children were also unclean because their mother was not circumcised, and they would have nothing to do with unclean children. This woman was financially capable of looking after the children, but the thought that she was responsible for the children being rejected by their father left her with an intense feeling of guilt. When asked if she would have her daughter circumcised, she said she was not sure. Her better judgment told her she should not. But, when she remembered what she had gone through in boarding school and in her marriage, she sometimes wondered whether it would be wise and fair for her to put her daughter through the same misery, considering that her society still believes strongly in female circumcision, and has no sympathy for a woman who does not conform.

The example of this Kenyan woman is given here because it is often difficult, even impossible for those who do not belong to a given culture, to fully appreciate the implications as well as the significance of aspects of that culture, and understand why even enlightened members of that society choose to conform against their better judgment.

Female circumcision is an issue that arouses very strong feelings in many women. Some Western feminists decry it because they feel that the principal objective of female circumcision, be it clitoridectomy, excision or infublation, is to suppress a woman's sexuality and make her docile and faithful to her husband - a clear example of how society ensures the subordination of women to men. Others, including African women from societies in which the practice does not exist, get horrified at the details of how the operation is performed. There is the risk of death from excessive bleeding or from tetanus or some other infection as a result of the operation, as well as the risk to a woman's health during childbirth on account of the scar that results from the operation. Some of the women who have been through the operation speak of how traumatic the whole experience was for them, and how they would not want to inflict such pain and emotional distress on their daughters. On the other hand, others are often irritated or even upset by the fuss that is made about it because they consider it a commonplace experience that women in their societies go through, just like circumcision in men.

In the societies that practise female circumcision, there are stories and beliefs that provide the rationale behind the practice. A little girl growing up in a village or in a suburb of an urban centre is bound to hear about these so many times that by the time she is of age she knows that the operation is for her own good, and that this is what she has to do to be accepted as a woman in her society, for the operation is usually meant to transform a girl into a woman.

Most African societies have procedures - initiation rites, puberty rites - that are meant to usher young boys and girls into adulthood. It is during such rites that young boys and girls are schooled by their elders on their rights and responsibilities as full citizens of their community, as well as their different roles as men and women in the home and in the society. These rites confer full social acceptability on the initiates, and, in traditional society, parents will ensure that their children participate in such initiation rites for fear of their being ostracised. Female circumcision, like male circumcision in some parts of Africa, is one such procedure.

It is obviously a very painful and dangerous procedure. Those who do not survive it have been bewitched or are accused of either being witches themselves, or of not being virgins at the time of the operation - a necessary prerequisite for a successful operation in some societies. For those who survive it, a happy celebration consisting in feasting and merry-making is assured, and they are showered with gifts, including expensive jewellry, by friends, relations and well-wishers. This is something for a girl to look forward to, and so the practice persists. An educated Gambian mother who refused to have her daughter circumcised found to her shock that her mother, concerned that her granddaughter would be a social outcast, took advantage of the girl's visit to her during her school holidays to have the operation performed on her, and what was worse, the girl came back with a sense of achievement.

There is no doubt that female circumcision is a grave health hazard to women, and every effort should be made to put an end to it. A law banning it will only help to push it underground and make it more difficult for those suffering from its effects to seek proper medical attention in the hospitals. Perhaps, like male circumcision, female circumcision should be seen as a necessary evil, particularly in those societies where it is a deeply rooted tradition, and regulations made to make it possible for it to be performed under proper medical conditions in hospitals. It should also be possible to provide training, like that given to traditional birth attendants, to those women who perform the operation, so as to reduce the health risk to the young girls.

Once the practice has been brought into the open, it should be possible to encourage a milder form of the operation so as to reduce the extent of scarring and other complications that pose problems for the woman in later life. For example, it is known that among the Mende of Sierra Leone, blood-letting is an important aspect of the operation. This aspect, which, for them has religious significance, can be preserved by a symbolic incision, without the need for total clitoridectomy. Such a procedure, which is aimed at preserving some significant aspect of the practice in the relevant society, is more likely to receive sympathetic consideration by those societies than an outright condemnation of the practice. Some Mende women do indeed opt for this symbolic operation. What is even more important is that any efforts at modification or eradication of the practice will have to come from women who are themselves members of these societies. Well-intentioned outsiders are likely to be looked at with suspicion, and accused of trying to undermine or destroy the culture of the society.

Efforts at modifying the operation should go hand in hand with education, of both young and old, on the risks that the operation poses for a girl both at the time of the operation and in later life. At the same time, every effort should be made to find other procedures for marking a girl's passage into adulthood, like those found in societies that do not practise female circumcision. For those girls who go through formal education, perhaps a big celebration at a convenient point in their education, preferably on completing school, so that they do not miss out on the merry-making and the gifts that are showered on them during this period. It should be possible for those in Christian communities to use the confirmation ceremony as the time for passing into adulthood both in the church and in the society, as is done in parts of Ghana. For non-Christians and for those who do not go through formal education, it should be possible to select an appropriate time after they have reached the age of puberty for a full-blown celebration. They may be kept in confinement for a few days during which grown-up women tell them all about womanhood, and inculcate in them the societal values of courage, endurance, fidelity, devotion to one's husband and so on, which are traditionally an essential part of initiation rites. At the end of the period, the girls can be brought out into the open with all the fanfare and festivities that are associated with passage into adulthood.

In order to ensure that such proposals for a viable alternative to female circumcision as an initiation rite are accepted, it would be necessary to have sustained discussion with, and education of traditional rulers and heads of village communities as well as of women's groups, to make them see the need for a change. They should also be encouraged to make suggestions as to the form the new initiation or puberty rites should take. Such a major exercise should not be the responsibility of a few concerned women's societies, but should be undertaken by both governmental and non-governmental agencies.

In a study done in Sierra Leone, "The Circumcision of Women, a Strategy for Eradication", Dr. Olayinka Koso-Thomas notes that the literate respondents in her sample wanted the practice discontinued because of their awareness of the health hazard it poses for both mother and child at the time of delivery. On the other hand, the non-literate respondents, both male and female, wanted the practice to continue because they felt its eradication would destroy a fundamental aspect of their culture. For them, this operation is important and necessary because it is what makes a woman accepted as a full adult member of her society, enjoying the rights and privileges that such status confers. It is clear, therefore, that formal education is a vital weapon in the fight against the practice, for it makes it easier for people to appreciate the health hazards that the operation poses for a woman. Moreover, education helps to expose the fallacies in the justification for it, such as the belief that it enhances fertility, or that it prevents still-births. This means that every effort should be made to increase the enrolment of girls in school. As has been suggested elsewhere, it is crucial that basic formal education be made available and accessible to both boys and girls in all countries if any headway is to be made in eradicating, or even modifying the traditional practices that continue to keep women in subordination in Africa.

To go back briefly to the reference made in the Introduction to the division of opinion on this subject at the Copenhagen Forum discussions, it can be seen that for the moment African women's concern about female circumcision has very little to do with the question of male superiority or the inequality of the sexes. However, although that concern has everything to do with its being a health hazard that needs to be eliminated, due cognizance is also taken of the cultural significance that the practice has for the relevant societies. African women, therefore, see the need, not only to fight against the practice on health grounds, but also to try and find a viable and acceptable alternative for it as an important and significant cultural event in the life of a young woman.

Chapter 2

PROMOTING WOMEN'S EMANCIPATION THROUGH SPECIFIC ACTIVITIES

In the preceding discussion of traditional practices that are obstacles to the emancipation of women in Africa, suggestions were made at various points as to how such practices may be modified or eliminated. In addition to measures such as government intervention in the form of legislation, it was observed that education, both formal and non- formal, as well as economic independence for women are major factors that can enhance the emancipation of women. In this chapter, we will look at specific educational and economic activities that were undertaken for women in Ghana which immensely enhanced the women's self-esteem and their participation in the economic and social life of their particular communities. Such participation also helped to make the women effective agents of change, especially in rural communities.

Although it is true to say that, in general, women in African societies are relegated to a rather subordinate position, throughout Africa, there are categories of women who command respect in their societies. These are women who wield a certain amount of power, usually in the political and religious fields; professional women who by virtue of their education and training hold responsible positions in the society, and wealthy women.

In some African societies, there are women who, as members of the ruling or royal family of their particular town or village, may become chiefs in their own right. Such women are given all the respect and status that is due to a traditional ruler. They are consulted on major issues affecting their community, and their views are respected.

Among the Zulu and the Swazi of Southern Africa, princesses are also accorded similar status in the society. Such hereditary position of authority is, however, not accessible to the majority of women. The status of such women is now more apparent in rural communities than in urban ones, where modern political systems and the authority of central governments, have considerably reduced the authority of traditional rulers. In modern times, the few women who hold responsible positions in the governments of their countries are accorded the same level of respect and status as their male counterparts. The number of such women is, however, small because in almost all African countries, the ability to express one's self effectively in English, French or Portuguese, the language of the former colonial power, is a necessary prerequisite for functioning effectively in Parliament and in politics at the national level. The low level of women's participation in formal education has, therefore, effectively limited the number of women who can hold responsible positions in government, or even participate meaningfully in the political life of their countries beyond the level of their local communities. There are also a few women who wield a considerable amount of power, especially in rural communities, as leaders of religious sects, or as diviners or oracles through whom the gods and/or ancestors transmit messages to the living. The number of such women too is, understandably, very small.

Professional women - lawyers, doctors, engineers, bankers, administrators and so on - command a great deal of respect in their countries. And it is true to say that, in general, a woman with the requisite training and expertise earns the same salary, has the same conditions of service, is accorded the same respect, and, to some extent, the same promotional opportunities in employment as her male counterpart. Such women often hold very responsible senior positions, and due respect is accorded them because they are known to be competent and efficient officers. In some West African societies, it is not unusual to hear such women being referred to in terms that may be loosely translated as 'woman-man' or 'a-woman-like-a-man', and this, not in derogatory terms, but with admiration. There is of course the usual tendency for men, and even women as well, to be unwilling to work under a woman boss. There is also the general feeling that a man needs money and a job or a promotion much more urgently than a woman does, and this misconception often leads to subtle forms of discrimination against women in employment, especially when it comes to promotion or appointment to very senior administrative or management positions. On the whole, however, professional women in Africa do not face the same level of discrimination in employment that women in similar positions have had to put up with in some Western countries. As stated earlier, they earn the same salaries and enjoy the same conditions of service as their male counterparts. Marriage and child-bearing do not mean an interruption in a woman's carreer, and the professional African woman does not need to put off child-bearing to a later date, when it may be too late, simply because she needs to establish herself in her carreer, a problem that many professional women face in the Western world. The discrimination that the professional African woman has to put up with is more within the home environment, where traditional attitudes about a woman's place in the home still persist. Indeed, there have been cases where working women have failed to take advantage of training programmes that are meant to upgrade their skills and thereby enhance their chances for promotion, because their husbands had refused to let them go. Usually, this is because the men felt they needed the women around to run the home, even in cases where the children were no longer very young.

The third group of women that society accords respect and status to are women who may or may not have had any formal education, but who by sheer dint of hard work and a shrewd business sense are able to provide adequately for themselves, their children and members of their extended family. The successful market women of West Africa fall into this category. They command the respect of members of their extended family, and are consulted on major issues affecting the family, and even the larger community in which they live. They are sought after by politicians, who need their financial support as well as their organizational ability for their political campaigns.

For the majority of African women, therefore, two viable avenues for enhancing their status in society are education and professional training on the one hand, and economic prosperity on the other. Formal education and professional training take a long time, and while it is available to girls, it excludes the large number of non-literate adult women in the society. For such women, respect and recognition comes mainly from their ability to contribute financially towards the well-being of the family and of the community in which they live. This group of women, mostly rural women, were the main target group for the Women in Development programmes and activities that were initiated in many African countries during the United Nations Decade for Women.

What follows in this chapter is a discussion of some of the programmes, projects and activities that the Ghana National Council on Women and Development (NCWD) initiated during the period 1975-1986 to increase the level of women's participation in public life at the local and national levels, to improve their access to formal education and professional training, and to improve their standard of living and their status in society by increasing their income-earning capacity. These activities were aimed at generating in women confidence in their own capabilities, enhancing their self-esteem and improving their status in their society by making them participate actively in, and contribute effectively to, the development of their individual communities and the nation as a whole. The activities discussed are mainly those whose impact was immediately evident. It must be pointed out, however, that in its role as an advisory body to government, the NCWD from time to time made recommendations to government on a number of issues affecting women, based on research findings and on concerns expressed at the seminars that were held from time to time with various groups of women in different parts of the country. Some of these recommendations had far-reaching implications for the status of women in the society. For example, the NCWD pointed out that the practice whereby women were not allowed to stand bail had no legal basis, and so was the provision in the passport application form that was introduced in the mid-70s which required a married woman to produce a letter of consent from her husband before she could be issued with a passport. Consequently, appropriate actions were taken on both issues. Action was also taken on the recommendation that all marriages, including Customary marriages, should be registered, when the law on the registration of marriages was passed in 1985, together with the Intestate Succession Law referred to in Chapter 1. It is not possible to discuss here the many NCWD recommendations and proposals that were aimed at improving the quality of life for women. These are published in the NCWD Annual Reports listed in the bibliography.

The NCWD was set up by the Ghana Government in 1975 to ensure that the objectives of International Women's Year and those of the United Nations Decade for Women are achieved in Ghana. It has a national secretariat and ten regional secretariats. All the staff are public servants paid by government, and the NCWD receives a budgetary allocation from government for its operations. In addition, it also receives grants from donor agencies for specific projects.

Women in Public Life

Ghana boasts of women in all the major professions: there are women lawyers, judges, doctors, engineers, pilots, University lecturers and professors, bankers, accountants, administrators and so on. These professional women have made, and are still making valuable contribution to various aspects of national life.

In spite of the increasing number of highly-qualified and competent women, the number of women in policy-making positions in government and on statutory bodies is very small. The NCWD decided to do something about this. At the time of its establishment, the country was under a military government, and it was explained that since there were no senior women army officers, it was not possible to have women in that government. The NCWD decided, therefore, to improve women's representation on the Boards of statal and para-statal bodies. A study of the membership of the various statutory bodies showed that less than 25 per cent of them had one woman on its board. The rest had none. A study of the educational background of the members revealed that about 35 per cent of them had no more than post-primary education, that is, no more than secondary school, teacher-training or technical education. The NCWD, therefore, made representations to government, pointing out that there were enough educated women in the country for there to be at least one-third women membership of all statutory bodies.

That government agreed to increase the representation of women on statutory bodies, and whenever the Boards of such bodies were to be reconstituted, the NCWD was asked to recommend names of qualified women to serve on them. Initially, the NCWD would contact the relevant women's professional organization - FIDA (the women lawyers association), Association of Women Dental and Medical Practitioners, Ghanaian Association of University Women, and so on, for names of people they thought could effectively serve on particular statutory boards. However, it became clear that a more efficient way of doing this was to compile a directory of women in the various professions, with details of their qualifications and experience. This was done, and copies sent to relevant government departments. Although it was never possible to have anything near one-third women membership of Boards, a conscious effort was made by that government and succeeding ones to have women representatives on statutory boards, and whenever it became necessary to revise the decree setting up a board, provision was made for there to be at least one woman member.

This particular activity of the NCWD considerably increased women's participation in policy- and decision-making at various levels, and it also exposed a number of women to broader national issues than they had been dealing with in their individual offices and departments. This had at least two observable results: it created a keen awareness among professional women of the numerous problems facing women in various aspects of national life. Following from this, it made it possible for these women to ensure that women's concerns were taken into account in making rules and regulations that governed the lives of women employed in the formal sector. One specific area in which such women's contribution affected the lives of many women employees is that of maternity leave. Women in Ghana are entitled to three months' paid maternity leave. They were normally expected to start their leave six weeks before confinement and resume work six weeks after. Some employers in the private sector insisted on a female employee starting work six weeks after the birth of her baby, and so if the child came earlier than expected, the mother still had to resume work six weeks after delivery, thus losing part of her three months' maternity leave entitlement. The employers did this to ensure that women did not give a false expected date of confinement in order that they would have more time at home after the birth of the baby, as was happening in some government departments.

As a result of the representation of women on the boards of many public establishments, it is now possible for a pregnant woman to postpone her annual leave and add it to her three months' maternity leave, so that she can spend a little more time with her infant baby, and also have time to make adequate and reasonably satisfactory child-care arrangements before she starts work.

As women on these boards tried to justify the need for such an amendment to the maternity leave provision, pointing out that it is impossible for a woman worker to concentrate on her job knowing that she has left a six-week-old baby at home who had probably not got used to bottle-feeding, they were struck by the way the men reacted when they realized the unreasonableness of the previous maternity leave terms. It became obvious to them that only women can effectively articulate women's concerns, and that there was an urgent need to have women on policy-making bodies. In some public institutions, it is now possible for a woman to take up to a year's leave of absence after the birth of her child, without loss of her job or seniority.

When in 1979 the country was poised for a third experiment in civilian government, the NCWD launched a programme to encourage women to stand for elections, and the result was encouraging. Five women were elected to represent their constituencies. This was the first time that a fairly large number of women had contested against men for parliamentary seats, and had been voted for in a general election. In the early 1960s, during the Nkrumah regime, the ruling Convention People's Party nominated six women to represent certain constituencies. In 1969, two women were elected to serve in Parliament during the general elections, so the election of five women in 1979 was quite an achievement for Ghanaian women in the political life of the country. However, when the government named the cabinet, there was not a single woman cabinet minister. Cabinet ministers in that government were selected by the President from outside Parliament, and the fact that no women ministers were appointed gave the impression that there were no women who qualified to serve in that position. There were, however, two Deputy Ministers. The NCWD made representations to the Government on this, pointing out that Ghana had had a woman Cabinet Minister during the First Republic 20 years before, and that the Government should seriously consider appointing women on to the cabinet. The government subsequently appointed one woman Minister to the Cabinet.

In the search for ways of promoting women's emancipation in Africa, the importance of competent women in policy-making positions at all levels cannot be over-emphasized. Such women can help initiate and ensure the implementation of programmes and activities that would promote the welfare of women, and encourage women's greater participation in national development. They can also provide the necessary insights into women's concerns that would ensure that government policies, projects and programmes have the desired impact and achieve the desired goals precisely because due account has been taken of the concerns and views of the different groups in the society. Moreover, it is clear that such women become effective role-models for the younger generation. It is to be hoped that African governments will become keenly aware of this and give their women effective positions on decision-making bodies.

Education

Women's education has always lagged behind that of men in all African societies, and there are several reasons for this. It has been explained that in traditional society, a major role for a woman is to ensure the continuity of the lineage, and she was expected to marry soon after puberty. She did not need formal education to perform this function. Moreover, a woman was expected to be provided for by her husband, and since education became a means for entering highly-paid jobs in the formal sector, it was considered more important for boys to have formal education, since they were to be the breadwinners in the family. In general, it is fairly easy for a girl with no formal education to make a living out of retail trade or the sale of snacks to workers. On account of this, most girls who started school did not continue beyond the primary school level. In a society where there are no social security benefits for old people, parents look on their children as their insurance against poverty in their old age. It did not seem profitable, therefore, to invest money in the education of a girl who was expected to get married and help her husband look after her children. For all these reasons, and also the fact that there was always the risk of a girl dropping out of school because of pregnancy, it was not considered important to invest money in a girl's education, and whenever money was short and a decision had to be made between keeping a son or a daughter in school, it was the daughter who was withdrawn. The practice still persists in rural communities. In urban centres, however, where the presence of successful professional women makes obvious the value of women's education, many parents now give every opportunity to their daughters to continue with their formal education to whatever level they are capable of.

In its efforts at improving the level of women's participation in formal education, the NCWD undertook a number of studies aimed at identifying the causes of the present low participation of girls in formal education and determining ways for dealing with these. An analysis that had been done (North et al 1975) of the 1973-74 educational statistics showed that although both boys and girls dropped out of school even from the first year of primary school, the highest drop-out rate for girls occurred between Class 3 and Class 6, when they were between 9 and 12 years of age. At this age, they were too young to make their own independent decision about the usefulness or otherwise of education to them, and they could not have dropped out of school as a result of pregnancy. It became clear, therefore, that one major reason for the low enrolment of girls in school is the fact that parents were not convinced of the value of girls' education.

It must be explained that, in 1960, the Government of Ghana made it a requirement for all children of school-going age to be sent to school, and fee-free education was instituted. However, parents are to pay a token fee for text-books and also buy school uniforms, so parents who cannot afford school uniforms, or who feel they need their children to take care of younger siblings, or help look after sheep and cattle and so on, withdraw the children from school at the earliest opportunity. The girls are particularly vulnerable,

50

for a girl may have to stay out of school to be a baby-sitter for younger siblings. After a series of such absence from school, she has difficulty in catching up with the rest of the class, and in due course she gives up school completely. Her trader mother feels she herself is doing very well in the market, and if all the girl needs education for is to be able to earn a decent income, then the earlier she starts learning to trade with her the better, so nobody tries to persuade her to continue with formal education.

Changing parental attitudes to girls' education is a very difficult task, given the apparent irrelevance of formal education to economic prosperity, especially for market women in urban centres. In recent years, however, the need to keep proper accounts for income tax purposes, and the obvious advantages gained by the ability to read and write especially when it comes to operating a bank account, are making parents keep their daughters in school, although most of them stop after Middle School, that is, after four years of post-primary education. Such girls have 10 years of formal education. With the introduction of the Junior and Senior Secondary School system, many of them stop their formal education at the end of the Junior Secondary School, which is three years of post-primary education.

The girls who complete secondary school (now Senior Secondary School) usually continue to train for a profession such as nursing, teaching, secretaryship and so on, or continue into university. However, the enrolment of girls in secondary and technical schools is rather low - about 30 per cent (1974/75 to 1985/86 statistics), and at this level pregnancy becomes an additional reason for girls dropping out of school. The percentage of female students in the three universities has also not changed much over the years - about 18 per cent. The main reason is that there are fewer secondary school places for girls than for boys, and it is the secondary schools that feed universities with students. Most secondary schools in Ghana are boarding schools, and while there are more boys' schools than girls' schools, the co-educational institutions usually provide one-third

51

boarding facilities for girls, thus effectively limiting the intake of girls. The NCWD found out that because of the limit on the intake of girls, one co-educational institution had a higher admission pass mark for girls than for boys at the Common Entrance Examination, the examination on which selection into secondary school was based, before the introduction of the Junior and Senior Secondary School system in 1987. This was obvious discrimination against women, and the NCWD pointed out that there was no reason why one dormitory block for boys could not be given to girls to bring equity into the admission requirements. No new dormitory block was allocated to girls, however. In recent years, the government policy of de-emphasizing the boarding aspect of secondary school education has meant that more girls can have access to secondary school education as day students. The full impact of this policy on girls' education is yet to be assessed.

Middle school leavers and secondary school leavers may train for one vocation or the other at a technical institute, a polytechnic, a commercial school or a vocational training centre. Here the girls are usually guided into what are considered female occupations - typing, secretaryship, catering, dressmaking, hairdressing and so on. Even where the opportunity exists for girls to train for 'non-female' jobs, girls do not apply for such training programmes. The NCWD was fortunate to have the co-operation of some heads of technical institutes who agreed to state specifically in their advertisements that girls may apply for any of the courses listed. One such institute, until then an all-male institute, agreed to reserve a number of places for girls if the NCWD could find suitable and willing students. The institute now regularly has female trainees. While on technical education, it must be said that government secondary technical schools, which offer technical rather than grammar school type liberal education, are for boys only, thus effectively limiting girls' access to such training.

One striking result of the consciousness-raising that

came with the programmes organized during the UN Decade for Women, was the way girls were prepared to venture into new areas of training hitherto reserved for men. There was a steadily-growing number of young women plumbers, auto-mechanics, radio-repairers and so on. The publicity given such girls in the media was also responsible for the increase in the number of girls who took up these occupations.

In the efforts to interest girls in these hitherto male occupations, it became clear that there is very little career guidance and counselling at all levels of the educational structure. The Ghana Education Service has a number of teachers trained to provide counselling services in schools, but the number is very inadequate. Moreover, because the teachers had classroom teaching responsibilities as well, they could not devote enough time to providing much needed counselling services to the students. Some non-governmental organizations (NGOs) and the universities from time to time went to secondary schools to advise students on which subjects were essential for certain specific careers. Rotary clubs in Ghana and the Ghanaian Association of University Women (GAUW) were two NGOs that had carried out this activity fairly consistently. The GAUW would organize 'Career Days' for girls in some secondary schools, at which the girls were told of career opportunities available to them and the training required for such careers. The NCWD assisted the Association with logistical support to run some of these programmes. However, it is obvious that such career counselling needs to be done on a regular basis as an integral part of school programmes. It is only in this way that boys and girls can be guided into and trained for occupations that are relevant to the development of the country. In this regard, an efficient establishment for manpower planning and development is an absolute necessity. Such an office should be able, at any given time, to provide adequate information on the manpower requirements of the country, indicating the skills and occupations that are needed, so that school leavers can be guided into, and trained in those skills that are relevant to, and essential for national development.

The need for vocational and professional training for female school-leavers was highlighted when a research study into the causes of mental disorder in a group of women in a suburb of Accra (Danquah, 1978) identified sexual harassment from male bosses and potential male employers as the second major cause, after poverty, of mental illness in those women. At a seminar where this and other research findings were discussed, two women told of cases they knew, of young girls, holders of the GCE Ordinary Level Certificate (the secondary school leaving certificate) who had been exploited by men who promised to give them employment. The men knew perfectly well that they were not in a position to give them any such employment, but they made these promises in order to have an affair with the girls. Secondary school education in itself does not provide a student with any specific skills, and girls who have only that qualification are, therefore, more likely to be exploited than those who have trained for skills that employers can use, such as typing, secretaryship, bookkeeping, plumbing, welding, catering and so on. This fact was frequently stressed at seminars, workshops and in the media, to make both parents and school girls appreciate the need for girls to train for one skill or the other after their basic education, so as to enhance their employment opportunities and reduce the risk of exploitation by unscrupulous men.

An important element in the promotion of women's education that was highlighted by a UNESCO-funded research into girls' access to higher education was that of effective role-models (Quarcoopome and Ahadji, 1981). Middle school girls in two locations - Bortianor, a fishing village near Accra, and in Somanya, a semi-urban setting in the Eastern Region of the country - were asked what their career aspirations were. Almost all the girls in Bortianor said they hoped to take up fish-smoking, the major economic activity of the women in the village. The girls in Somanya, on the other hand, had a variety of careers in mind. Some

54

hoped to become doctors, nurses, teachers, lawyers, welfare officers and so on, while others wanted to be traders and farmers. The Primary and Middle schools in Bortianor had not had female teachers for many years, and the exposure of the girls to educated professional women was extremely limited. Bortianor is a popular beach resort, and the girls must have come into contact with a number of educated women who came to the beach at weekends, but it is clear that they looked on them as city women, and could not identify with them. Parents in Bortianor who wanted their daughters to have higher education usually sent them to Accra to live with a relation, for they were fully aware of the lack of ambition of the girls who had all their formal education in the village. The girls in Somanya, on the other hand, either had relations who were professional women, or knew a number of such women who were citizens of Somanya or who lived and worked in the town.

This research showed that girls in rural areas are doubly disadvantaged. They have to leave their village if they want to have higher education, and they have no role-models who can effectively open their minds to the variety of careers that are available to women in the country. It is not surprising, therefore, that the dropout rate for girls, due to pregnancy or just lack of interest, was very high in the Bortianor Middle School; the girls did not need to finish school to become efficient at fish-smoking. The NCWD could not do much about the first problem, but it tried to identify successful professional women in the different regions of the country, and such women were often invited to speak to women's groups or chair functions in villages, so that they could be role-models for the girls.

As far as non-formal education is concerned, Ghana had a vigorous literacy programme in the 1950s, organized by the Department of Social Welfare and Community Development. When compulsory fee-free primary education was introduced in 1960, it was assumed that in due course all young people would have formal education, and by the end of the 1960s the literacy programme had lost its momentum. It has been pointed out that the compulsory, fee-free primary education did not achieve the desired results since many children did not stay long enough in school to be able to read and write. Adult literacy programmes are now being actively pursued by the Department of Community Development, the Non-Formal Education section of the Ministry of Education, the Institute of Adult Education, University of Ghana, and by some non-governmental bodies such as the Ghana Institute of Linguistics, Literacy and Bible Translation. The NCWD had the co-operation of these institutions in organizing functional literacy classes for some of the women in the women's groups that have been organized around specific economic activities. The women are taught to read and write in their own languages. The results of the programme have been very encouraging, for the ability to read and write has given the women added self-confidence and has increased their self-esteem.

The importance of education to the emancipation of women cannot be overemphasized. It is ignorance that has made women accept the inferior position to which they have been relegated by society for centuries. Spurious beliefs about a woman's subordinate position based on cultural and religious concepts that cannot stand up to close scrutiny, as well as misconceptions about her physiology and her intelligence have made women accept without question the superiority of men. Moreover, such beliefs and misconceptions have made women feel generally inadequate and incapable of functioning effectively in society at the same level as men. Only education can foster in women an analytical and a critical mind that would make them question the religious, cultural and physiological bases of their supposed inferiority. Only education can give women knowledge that would expose the fallacies behind the cultural practices that keep them in subordination. Without such education being made available to girls, the emancipation of African women will take several more centuries, consequently heightening the contrast between educated urban citizens and illiterate rural communities, a contrast which poses a real threat to social stability. Social conflict in Africa is as likely to arise out of the difference in the perception and understanding of social, cultural and national issues because of a difference in educational background, as much as it is likely to arise out of the inequality in the distribution of wealth. African governments, therefore, owe it to their people to make basic education available and accessible to all their citizens to ensure that the majority of the population living in the rural areas can participate effectively in, and contribute meaningfully to national development. One can only hope that the economies of African countries will, in the not-too-distant future, be such as can support at least nine years of compulsory and free basic education for all children. It is only through such a programme that true emancipation for African women, especially rural African women, can be ensured.

Income-generating Activities

Soon after its establishment in 1975, the NCWD organized a series of consultations with women's organizations in all the regions of the country, to find out from Ghanaian women what they perceived as their most immediate concerns to which priority attention must be directed. The response from all over the country was clear: the women wanted to be able to earn enough money so that they could feed, clothe and generally take better care of their children. This was the period when Ghana was suffering from the effects of the Sahelian drought, and the country's economy was in a sore state. Those in the rural areas also wanted government to provide them with good drinking water and health posts within easy reach.

Traditionally, a woman on marriage may be given money by her husband as capital with which she is expected to trade or to start whatever income-generating activity she chooses so that she can provide her own basic needs and those of her children. Children's school fees and other major expenditure, such as housing, is usually the responsibility of the husband. In farming communities, in addition to working on her husband's farm, a woman usually has her own piece of land on which she grows vegetables and staple foods for feeding the family. The money she earns from the extra produce that she sells is what she spends on some of her basic needs and those of her children.

With the economic decline in the country, primarily as a result of low commodity prices on the world market, it became increasingly obvious that in many homes, the man's income alone could not support the family. The urgent need for women to earn enough money to supplement the family income was reinforced when a couple of years later, research into the causes of mental disorder in a group of women from a suburb of Accra (Danquah, 1978) identified poverty (inadequate house-keeping money) as the highest single cause of mental disorder among them. The NCWD, therefore, had to make the improvement of women's income-generating activities its priority concern, in order to meet this felt need of Ghanaian women. Workshops were organized throughout the country to identify the income-generating activities that women were engaged in, to find out what the constraints were, be they capital, availability of inputs such as raw materials for soap-making, basket weaving, pottery, etc.; absence of appropriate technology to lighten the work-load of the women, increase their output and, in some cases such as in food-processing, upgrade the quality of the end product; marketing and so on, and efforts were made to find solution to these problems. These workshops brought to light valuable information that was not generally available. For example, it was at one such workshop that the NCWD learnt that the ashes of the fibrous waste that was thrown away, after palm nuts have been removed from the bunch, was a very good source of potash, which, together with palm oil or palm kernel oil is used in making a type of local soap that is black or dark grey in colour. The better-known sources of potash were the ashes of plantain peels which could only be collected in small quantities at a time, and the ashes of cocoa pods, which were seasonal - only during the cocoa harvest. This information became the basis for the establishment of a potash-processing plant near a palm-oil-processing factory on an oil palm plantation at Kwamoso, in the Eastern Region. The project was funded by the United States Agency for International Development (USAID). The processed potash was sold to women in Koforidua, the Eastern Regional capital, and in the surrounding villages, in packets with instructions on how to make the local soap.

At another workshop, a woman came with a very attractive basket woven with the fronds of the date palm. She told of how, in the early 1960s, the Nkrumah Government had brought into the country Chinese craftsmen to teach women from Dabala in the Volta Region, how to make baskets with date palm fronds, for date palm trees are common in the area. That Government built a centre for training women in the area in basket weaving, but the project was abandoned after the overthrow of the Nkrumah Government in 1966. She said that there were four of them who still made the baskets, and she was willing to teach anyone who would like to learn the skill. As a result of this workshop, the NCWD sought funding from the International Planned Parenthood Federation, renovated the building and started a training programme in basket weaving for young women in Dabala and nearby villages. Three of the four women who had been trained by the Chinese were engaged to train the young women.

Perhaps the most valuable outcome of these workshops is the fact that they provided a forum for the exchange of ideas among women from different parts of the country. They also made it possible to collect information about new techniques for carrying out various activities, for it became clear that women in different parts of the country had slightly different ways of doing similar things, or used the same raw materials in producing different things for sale. Fortunately, the women were usually very willing to teach others their particular way of doing things, and such women became resource persons at workshops where specific skills were taught.

It soon became clear that unlike women in the rural areas, women in the urban centres, who normally engage in petty trading, were mainly interested in income-generating activities that had a quick turnover. They were also not very keen on working with others in co-operatives. For such women a workshop was organized at which women from different ethnic groups in the country were invited to exhibit different types of snacks that are prepared from local foodstuffs like maize, cassava (manioc), ripe and unripe plantain, yam, cocoyam, millet, guinea corn, rice, beans, groundnuts, tigernuts, etc., as well as drinks and other preparations from local fruits. The result was impressive. Nobody at the workshop had imagined that such a wide range of snacks could be prepared from these foodstuffs. This was the time when wheat flour, which is imported, and which most caterers prefer, was expensive and hard to come by. The aim was to expose young women in particular to the variety of snacks that they can prepare and sell to workers and school children, for such activity does not involve much capital, and there is always a ready market. This was one of the most successful workshops, for the impact it made was immediate. The young women could now engage in a lucrative activity which was, in many cases, more profitable than petty trading in manufactured goods, which were not readily available at the time. Where necessary, especially with those using maize, rice and flour as their raw materials, the women were organized into groups in different sections of the urban centres, and their leaders helped to obtain regular supplies at controlled prices from the Ghana Food Distribution Corporation.

It was with rural women that the NCWD was able to initiate major income-generating projects involving the use of appropriate technology. A few of these are discussed below. It must be emphasized, however, that each income-generating project was an integrated educational programme involving lectures and practical demonstration

60

on nutrition, child-care, family planning, sanitation, civic responsibilities such as the payment of taxes and so on. In some areas it was also possible to start literacy classes for the women. Some of the more general topics discussed at the seminars and lectures were on the role of women in a changing society; vocational training and job opportunities for women; women's health and diseases, such as breast cancer, that are peculiar to women; how to deal with the adolescent child; traditional practices and their effect on the status of women; the contribution of women to national development, and so on. These were aimed at giving women a broader outlook, as well as creating in them a keen awareness of national issues and of problems facing women in the country, and possible ways of dealing with them. In addition, women who had made a success of their careers, such as farmers, traders, queenmothers, nurses, teachers, welfare officers and so on were identified in the various regions of the country, and women's groups were encouraged to invite them to speak at their monthly meetings. Such women became very effective role-models for, especially, the younger women. The income-generating activities therefore became a vital element in the NCWD's efforts at promoting women's emancipation and improving their status in society.

Agriculture

Farming is a major activity of women living in the rural areas. Most of the women have small farms on which they grow staple foods and vegetables primarily for feeding the family, but they sell the extra produce to supplement the family income. The women have full control of the money they earn. There are women entrepreneurs who do commercial farming, usually of maize or oil palm, but these are very few.

The NCWD identified access to land and access to credit as the major problems facing small-scale women farmers.

61

While women entrepreneurs can obtain lease on large acreage of land to do commercial farming, and they also can provide the necessary collateral to obtain loans from the banks to hire tractors and labour, the small-scale farmer had no collateral and was not in a position to expand her farm.

The staff of the NCWD's regional secretariats helped these small-scale farmers to overcome their handicap. The vegetable growers were the first to be helped. These farmers grow tomatoes, garden eggs, pepper and okra. The capital they needed to operate efficiently was very small, and some of them had been relying on the market women from the urban centres, who came to buy their produce, to pre-finance them. This sometimes resulted in a dependency relationship, with the farmer not having the freedom to sell to any other person than the one who pre-financed her.

The NCWD set up a revolving fund from which small loans were given to the women before the planting season, to help them pay for labour and also to tide them over till the harvest. In some cases, women whose farms were adjacent to each other contributed a small amount of money each for their land to be cleared and ploughed together by the Mechanization Unit of the Ministry of Agriculture, for, individually, their farms were too small to be so prepared. Officers of the Agricultural Extension Unit gave the women improved seeds for planting, and generally gave advice on when and how to plant for the best results. After the harvest, the women promptly repaid the loans, and the repayment rate was almost 100 per cent at the end of the first year of the operation of the revolving fund.

The impact of the scheme was very evident, especially on those farmers who had been relying on market women to pre-finance them. They were no longer beholden to anybody, and could confidently go to the market centres and sell their produce at the going price. This meant more income for the family, and a general improvement in their standard of living.

Encouraged by the success of the scheme, the NCWD

staff approached chiefs in the relevant towns and villages for land for the women, so that they could expand their farms. The chiefs were very willing to do this, and the women were organized into groups, around particular crops, to farm on the land released by the traditional rulers. Now that the women had a much larger acreage to farm, it was possible for them, as a registered group, to obtain loans from the banks to have the land cleared and prepared for planting, and to pay for needed labour. The land was usually divided equally among the particular group of women farmers, and each farmed her own land and harvested her crop.

It had been clear from the beginning that running co-operative farms on which a group of women worked together, harvested together and shared the profit after the sale of the produce would not work, for there would always be the suspicion that one or the other member of the co-operative was not putting in as much time and energy as the others. Moreover when the women worked independently on their individual farms, they could always get help from members of their extended family.

During the period between planting and harvesting, the women were taught other skills such as the making of handicrafts with raw materials that are readily available in their area, in order to help them improve their income-earning capacity.

After the harvest and sale of the produce, each woman farmer paid back her share of the bank loan, and again the repayment rate was almost 100 per cent. Each woman farmer also contributed a pre-determined amount of money into a common fund for the group so that they could build up the necessary capital for the next planting season. There usually was not much problem with the sale of the produce because market women from the urban centres would come and buy truck-loads of the produce to sell. The only problem was with transportation, for the women had to carry head-loads of their produce from their farms to the main road before they could find transport to convey the foodstuffs to the nearest market centre. Sometimes, it was possible to hire a tractor to transport the produce from the farms, but this means of transportation was not always available. Transportation, therefore, remains a major problem for, especially, the vegetable growers, whose crops are too seasonal (farming is still dependent on the weather, rather than on irrigation) for them to consider as necessary and feasible, the huge investment that is needed to acquire a tractor.

There were two farming projects which were big enough for the problem of transportation to be effectively tackled. These were at Damongo in the Northern Region, and at Mafi-Kumasi in the Volta Region. The Damongo project was basically a cassava-growing project, while the Mafi-Kumasi project was an integrated cassava-growing and gari-processing project. Both are discussed below in some detail. The Mafi-Kumasi project was funded by the USAID, which provided a factory and a tractor. The Mafi-Kumasi women's co-operative was able to buy a second tractor with a bank loan from Adidome Rural Bank, the first such loan to be given by the bank at the beginning of its operations. The Damongo cassava-growing project was, however, funded by the women themselves with a bank loan.

Damongo is in the Northern Region of Ghana. Many women in this area grow cassava and a few of them process it into gari. Women from eight localities in the Damongo area were organized into a registered farmers' co-operative. The chiefs in the area were approached to release more land for the women to expand their farms, and this they willingly did. The farmers' co-operative started an account with the local bank, and after a year, they were able to obtain a bank loan for the purchase of two tractors. This was an extraordinary achievement, for this is a rural community in a patrilineal, extremely male-dominated society. The women would never have dared approach the bank for such assistance if they had not been motivated and encouraged by the NCWD Regional Secretary and her staff. This is a clear example of how effective well-trained and highly motivated field staff can be in promoting the necessary self-confidence

64

and drive that are essential to the emancipation of women. The NCWD Regional Secretary realized that the quality of gari produced by the women was not as good as that produced by women in some other parts of the country. She, therefore, arranged with the NCWD Regional Secretary of the Brong Ahafo Region, immediately south of the Northern Region, for some of the Damongo women to visit gari processors in that region to learn how they made the better-quality gari. The NCWD was subsequently able to provide them with gari-processing equipment through Technologies for Rural Women, a project funded by the Netherlands Government.

The Damongo cassava-growing and gari-processing project was one of the successful integrated projects. Its success does not primarily lie in the fact that it increased the women's income-earning capacity, or that it removed the drudgery in the farming and gari-making procedures by the provision of tractors and gari-processing equipment. Its success really lies in the self-confidence that it has given the women, and in the way it has raised their level of consciousness and made them aware of their own capabilities. It also lies in the respect that such economic success, and the resulting financial contribution that the women can make to the development of their community, has brought them from both men and women in their community, for it has made it possible for their voice to be heard in discussions on matters affecting the community. This is no small achievement for, as has been stated earlier, Damongo is in a patrilineal male-dominated traditional society.

Food Processing

The processing and preservation of food, be it farm produce or fish, has always been a women's activity in Ghana. Some of the food-processing activities are the extraction of edible oil from the palm fruit, palm kernel, coconut, groundnut and shea nut; the dehydration of root crops and vegetables such as cassava (manioc), pepper and okra; the processing of cassava into gari, a coarse-grain pre-cooked preparation made from grated cassava, pressed dry of sap, and dehydrated by roasting; and the preservation of fish by smoking, drying or salting.

The major problems facing women engaged in these activities were access to simple appropriate technology that would relieve them of the drudgery involved in their food processing procedures. They also needed capital that would enable them to buy raw materials in sufficiently large quantities so as to reduce cost. Women who are engaged in these activities, like women farmers, work on their own with the assistance of their children and members of their extended family.

What follows is a discussion of specific food-processing and food-preservation activities undertaken with and for rural women, and the impact these activities had on the women's own self-esteem and their status in their respective communities.

The Mafi-Kumasi Gari-processing Project

Mafi-Kumasi is one of a cluster of eighteen villages in the Mafi Traditional Area in the Volta Region. The women have cassava farms but their main occupation is the processing of cassava into gari. This is a very tedious process involving the grating of the peeled cassava, after which the dough is put into sacks and water pressed out of it by placing huge stones on the sacks for about two days. The dry cassava meal is broken up into a powdery form and then roasted in a wide steel pan over a slow fire until cooked and dry.

USAID provided funds for the construction of a model gari-processing factory for the women of this area. The women were organized into a women's co-operative that would own and operate the factory. The factory was a gift, and the women were not expected to contribute anything

66

towards the purchase and installation of the equipment. The NCWD pointed out to the funding agency that it would be desirable for the women to pay a percentage of the cost of the factory to ensure their commitment to the project. The money paid by them could be used in helping other women's groups in the area. This was not acceptable to the agency, for they pointed out that the money for the project was a grant.

In order to ensure a regular supply of cassava to feed the factory, USAID provided a tractor to help the women expand their cassava farms, and the chiefs willingly gave land for the purpose. The women bought a second tractor with a loan from the nearby Rural Bank at Adidome.

The factory was built, and the equipment installed. It consisted of a mechanical grater, a press, sieves, improved roasting pans and commercial scales for weighing the cassava as well as the finished product. Smokeless ovens which had been designed by the Home Economics Division of the Ministry of Agriculture Extension Unit were built for roasting the gari. A KVIP toilet (Kumasi Ventilated Improved Pit latrine) designed by the Engineering Department of the University of Science and Technology, Kumasi, was built at the factory, and it became a model for the villages around to construct similar ones to replace the traditional open pit latrines used in rural areas. A tank was built to store rain water so as to ensure a constant supply of water at the factory. The village did not have pipe-borne water.

The Mafi-Kumasi gari-processing project was the first major project of the NCWD, and its implementation provided a very useful learning experience. It has been discussed here to show what can go wrong with a well-intentioned, well-planned project, and also to show how the lessons learnt from it guided the operation of subsequent projects.

The first difficulty the NCWD encountered was with the men in the area. Serious discussions about the formation of the Co-operative was started with the women, but soon afterwards some men came to protest that they would not allow their wives to join the Co-operative unless they also became members. The men owned cassava farms from which the women bought additional cassava for processing into gari. The men were promised that they would have access to the tractor that was coming with the project, so that they could expand their farms and earn more money, but this was not acceptable to them. The fear of their losing control over their wives if the women earned more money than they, could not be so easily set aside. In the end, it was decided to allow a few men into the Co-operative, but that their number should not exceed one-third of the total membership. Other conditions were that the President, Vice-President and Secretary of the Co-operative had to be women. After resolving that issue, the next problem was to persuade the funding agency to accept this amendment, for the project was meant to be an all-women's Co-operative. Eventually, the membership of the men was accepted. The Co-operative had 175 members.

The factory was officially commissioned in 1980 by the then Head of State, President Hilla Limann, amid a lot of fanfare. The American Ambassador and officials of USAID were also present. The women wore their white overalls and demonstrated how gari could now be processed in a matter of hours. They were proud to be the centre of attraction, and were thrilled at the thought that it was because of them that the President of the Republic had visited their village. It was clear that their men were also proud of them. Although the grater and the press could have been operated by women, on account of the male membership in the Co-operative, the men had convinced the women that those two pieces of machinery could not be operated by women, and so two young men worked the grater and the press.

For one year, the factory operated successfully, and schools and other institutions found it convenient to go there for their bulk purchases of gari since they could obtain the quantities they needed in one place. The Co-operative had an account at the nearby Rural Bank at Adidome where proceeds from the operation of the factory were saved.

During the first year, the NCWD stationed a staff member at Mafi-Kumasi to manage the factory and train his assistant, a local young woman who had been sent on a course in management. She was to take over from him. At the end of the year, the NCWD staff member was withdrawn and the young woman took over.

It soon became clear that there were two major problems with the project. The first was that because the women had not invested any money of their own in the project, they did not quite feel that *they* owned it, and that it was their responsibility to ensure that it functioned efficiently. They felt that was the responsibility of the NCWD. The other problem was with the organization of the Co-operative itself. These were women who had been processing and selling gari on their own for years, and they were suspicious about putting their money into a common fund and waiting for their share of the profits at a later date when the accounts of the Co-operative had been finalized. Some of the women subsequently refused to bring their cassava to be processed at the factory. Those who did, paid for the use of the equipment, as was done by non-members of the Co-operative.

This second problem seemed insurmountable, and it was eventually decided, with the members, that each individual, members and non-members alike, who used the equipment at the factory should pay a fee, to be determined by the members. The money should be paid into their Co-operative account at the bank, and used to maintain and repair the equipment. The same procedure was to be followed with the use of the tractor.

It must be said, however, that as far as saving the women the time and the drudgery involved in gari-processing was concerned, the project was very successful. The same can be said of making it possible for the women to increase their income and thereby being able to better feed and clothe themselves and their children. The Co-operative also became a viable group for educating the women on sanitation, nutrition, child-care, family planning and so on. But the objective of promoting in these rural women the self-

69

confidence that comes with owning, managing and controlling a project of this size was not achieved. The lessons that were learnt from this project, however, helped in the implementation of subsequent ones.

Essam Oil-Processing Project

Essam is a small village in the Eastern Region of Ghana. The village is in an oil-palm-growing area. The men own the farms, and the major economic activity of most of the women is the processing of palm fruits into palm oil, and the kernels into palm kernel oil. The women usually buy the fruits from the men, do the oil-processing individually at home and sell the oil in the main market centre in the nearby district capital, Akim Oda.

In the late 1960s, a teacher of the Ghana Education Service, who had been trained in the making of bar soap, was posted to Essam to teach soap-making in the Essam Continuation School. Continuation schools provided, for middle school pupils who did not continue into secondary school, two years training in crafts and other economic activities that are meant to enable the trainees to become self-employed. The crafts taught were based on the raw materials available in the immediate vicinity of the town or village where the school is located. Essam was a good place for making soap because of the availability of palm oil and palm kernel oil, the major raw material for soap-making. The other raw material needed was caustic soda, which had to be bought from the urban centres.

The teacher, Mr. J.D. Oduro, decided to use his spare time teaching the women how to make bar soap, for, when the oil palm harvest was good, they often had difficulty selling the large quantities of palm oil and the palm kernel oil that they had processed. Some of the women were already making a type of local soap made from palm oil and potash. Mr. Oduro had married the daughter of the queenmother of Essam, and with the queenmother's support, he was able to organize a

70

group of about twenty women for his soap-making class.

Mr. Oduro was also a member of the People's Educational Association which, in addition to organizing remedial
classes for school leavers who wish to re-sit certain school-
leaving examinations, organizes adult literacy classes.
Having won the confidence of the women with the success of
the soap-making classes, he decided to teach them to read
and write. Only one member of the group had had primary
school education, and she was made secretary/treasurer of
their little group.

The Eastern Regional Secretariat of the NCWD was
approached by the Essam soap-making group for assistance
in obtaining caustic soda which they bought at a rather high
price in small quantities from retailers. They had no
problem with the sale of the soap they produced, for there was
always a ready market.

The NCWD National Secretariat in Accra had already
established contact with the Ministry of Trade, and had an
allocation of imported caustic soda, which the regional
secretariats distributed to various soap-making women's
groups throughout the country. It was, therefore, not difficult
for the Essam group to obtain their caustic soda supply from
the Eastern Regional Secretariat.

The NCWD National Secretariat was told about the
Essam soap-making group, and after a visit by its Projects
Committee, it was decided to help the women obtain oil-
extraction equipment to reduce the drudgery involved in
their palm-oil-processing procedures, and to expand their
operations, for there was an abundant supply of palm fruits
in the area. The NCWD was at the time having discussions
with the Ghana representative of the Netherlands Government about the funding of Technologies for Rural Women, a
project that was to be implemented under the auspices of the
United Nations International Labour Organization (ILO).
The NCWD decided to add Essam to the list of rural
women's groups that should benefit from the project.

The Chief of Essam and his elders were informed about
the NCWD's decision, and a request was made for land on

71

which the oil-extraction equipment was to be installed. The land was given. It was explained to them that although the equipment was to be provided free by the Netherlands Government, the women would have to pay the equivalent of one-third the cost of the equipment and its installation, so that that money could be used to help other groups of women who were not as lucky as they were. The women agreed to this, and so did the funding agency. Experience with the Mafi-Kumasi project had shown that the success of such a project depended on a high level of commitment on the part of the women involved. Such commitment would be forthcoming only if the women had a stake in the success of the project. When they have committed money to a project, they will work to recoup it, and that is the only way one can ensure the success of a project. The oil-extraction equipment was initially made up of two boilers for the palm fruit, a pounder, two oil presses and a clarifying tank. Later a nut-cracker was added for the palm kernels. All these were bought from the Technology Consultancy Centre (TCC) of the University of Science and Technology, Kumasi. They were installed in a shed that had been constructed on the land given by the chief. A staff member from the TCC taught the women how to operate the various pieces of equipment, so they did not have to employ anybody for the purpose. A soap-making tank was added to complete the set of equipment the women needed.

The Mafi-Kumasi experience had made it clear that Ghanaian women who have been working independently for years are not happy about working with others in a strict co-operative system, in which all their money went into a common fund, and so the women were allowed to work out their own system of operation. They decided that in order to raise the money they needed for the one-third of the total cost that they had to refund, each member would every week provide a quantity of palm nuts which they would process into edible oil or into soap. The proceeds from the sale of the oil and/or soap would go into a common fund. They had started a bank account in the district capital, Akim Oda. The rest of the time, each member could go there to process her fruits at a small fee. The fee was what they planned to use for maintaining and repairing the equipment. Other women in the village who did not belong to the group could use the equipment to process their fruits, but at a slightly higher fee.

When the Essam project started functioning, the women increased their palm-oil production to such an extent that the NCWD had to make arrangements for two women's soap-making groups in other parts of the Eastern Region, where palm oil was not plentiful, to obtain their supply of palm oil from Essam.

The success of the project did not, however, lie primarily in increasing the women's income-earning capacity. It was in the self-confidence that it generated in the women. These were women in a small village, who had never had any formal education. They had always known that it is men who operate machines, and educated men at that. For them to be able to operate the oil-extraction equipment was something they could never have imagined possible, and the excitement on their faces as they worked these machines was a joy to see. They had broken the myth about the innate non-intelligence of illiterate men and women, as well as the myth about the inability of women to understand how machines work. The men in the village were impressed by, and proud of their women. The confidence the project gave the women was very obvious when one compared the way they stood up to ask questions or express an opinion at meetings we had with them after the implementation of the project, with the way they had had to be prompted and encouraged to speak at the initial stages of the project. These women were truly emancipated in a way in which no number of lectures on the equality of the sexes and a woman's innate abilities could have accomplished.

Having won the confidence of the women as a result of the success of the project, the NCWD had no difficulty in getting their co-operation for the various educational programmes that it organized for them - discussions on nutrition, child-care, sanitation, family-planning, the need to send their children to school, and to fulfil their civic responsibilities such as paying their taxes. The literacy classes continued, and some of them, after being able to read and write in their own language, expressed the wish to start learning English. This project became the model for subsequent similar projects.

The project was, of course, not without its problems. When the men learnt that the women were going to be given oil-extraction equipment, some of them became jealous, and very nervous about the women making more money than they. It is the general belief among Ghanaian men that when a woman makes too much money, she no longer gives her husband the respect that is due to him. From the Mafi-Kumasi experience, the NCWD knew that it was important to win the support of the men if the project was to succeed, so right from the start, the discussions about the project were held at meetings where both the men and the women were present. The men asked why only the women were being singled out for assistance, and it became clear that we had to involve them in some way, for if they refused to let their wives join the group, there would be no project. The men oil-palm growers were, therefore, helped to form an association so that they could have access to the services of the Extension Unit of the Ministry of Agriculture. As individuals, their farms were too small to attract the attention of the extension officers.

A final point that must be made about the Essam project is how much one dedicated individual can achieve in motivating people and bringing out their potential. Mr. Oduro had already got a group organized before the NCWD came on the scene. Since he was married, and to a woman from the village, the men were prepared to allow their wives to join his soap-making group and attend the literacy classes. After the project had become fully operational, he one day organized an excursion to Accra, the nation's capital, for the women. He took them to interesting places in Accra and Tema, including the International Airport and the Tema Harbour, where they were taken round a ship. To crown it all, the women had about 20 minutes' flight in an Air Force plane at the Air Force Base. Mr. Oduro had made these arrangements on an earlier visit to Accra. When, at the end of their tour, the women visited the offices of the NCWD, it was clear that their self-esteem had gone up so much higher by their experience in the aeroplane. Now they knew that there was hardly anything that a non-literate village woman could not do if she put her mind to it.

These are liberated women. It does not matter if some of them, especailly the older ones, still call their husbands 'Miwura' (my master). It does not matter if some still have to take turns to live with their husbands because they are in a polygamous marriage. What matters is that they have succeeded in shedding off those inhibitions that make them have very little confidence in their own capabilities. Now they know what they are capable of, and in that knowledge lies the essence of their liberation. They now have the confidence to express their views on matters affecting their community, and they know they will be listened to because they now contribute financially to the development of their community. What is even more important, they can now make decisions on matters affecting their own lives, such as how many children they themselves want to have, not how many their husbands want them to have. They also know their husbands will take note of what they say because their money helps in paying the children's school fees. Moreover, the men know they cannot threaten the women with divorce over such an issue for they know the women are capable of looking after themselves and their children. What had started as a pure economic venture, turned out to be an effective means for promoting the emancipation of these rural women.

The Fish-smoking Project

Fish-curing is a major economic activity of women living along the coast, near major rivers such as the Volta, and on the banks of the man-made Volta lake and the crater lake, Lake Bosomtwi. The women buy the fish from the fishermen and preserve it by smoking, sun-drying or salting. Such cured fish can keep for months if it is properly stored and aired at regular intervals. The cured fish is bought by market women and sold throughout the country. Because the greater part of sea-fishing is done by canoe fishermen who cannot do deep-sea fishing, fish in Ghana is seasonal, and during the lean season, the price of fish goes up, and fishmongers make a substantial amount of money from the sale of smoked or salted fish. There are cases where the women have been able to buy canoes or fishing nets for the men to work with, and they, therefore, earn additional money as owners of canoes or fishing nets.

Fish-smoking is traditionally done on a wooden rack or wire mesh on top of a circular mud oven about one metre from the ground. During the fishing season, the women, especially in the rural areas, stay up all night smoking layer after layer of fish before it goes bad, for there are no refrigeration facilities in these areas. Sometimes during the herring season, fishermen in the villages go through the frustrating experience of having to throw fish back into the sea for lack of cold-storage facilities.

Fish is the main source of animal protein in Ghana, and the NCWD identified fish-smoking as one of the major income-generating activities whose operation can be considerably improved and made more efficient by the introduction of simple technology. Kokrobite, a fishing village near Accra, was chosen as the site for a pilot project, and a new fish-smoking kiln designed by the Department of Fisheries was introduced to a group of women. After trying the kiln for a couple of months, the women rejected it because they said it was not very suitable for their purposes. One thing was clear, however: the design of the kiln was so different from anything that they were familiar with that they had difficulty in getting used to it. Moreover, although the kiln was a more hygienic way of smoking fish, the quantities the women smoked with it were not as dramatic an improvement on their traditional methods as was the case with the gari-processing and oil-extraction equipment, and the women were, therefore, not too keen on continuing with it.

In the meantime, the NCWD had heard about a new fish-smoking technology, designed by the Food Research Institute of the Council for Scientific and Industrial Research in Ghana, which was successfully being used by the women of Chorkor, a suburb of Accra. The Chorkor oven, as it became known, had been designed by the Food Research Institute in close collaboration with the women of Chorkor. It is designed on the same principle as the traditional fish-smoking oven, but with a few innovations. The mud (or now sandcrete) oven is rectangular, not circular in shape, and about half a metre from the ground. The rack on which the fish is smoked is made of a sheet of rectangular wire mesh, the same measurements as the top of the sandcrete oven. The mesh is bounded on the four sides with wooden batons in such a way that when several trays are stacked one on top of the other on the sandcrete oven, they act as a chimney through which smoke from the firewood below travels upwards, smoking and drying the layers of fish on the trays in the process. This means that the women can smoke several layers of fish at a time, between four and twelve layers, using the same fuel. The number of layers depends on the size of the fish - the smaller the fish, the more the layers. From time to time, the women rotate the layers of fish, bringing the top trays to the bottom to ensure that all the layers are evenly smoked and dried.

This new process that made it possible for large quantities of fish to be smoked at a time, saved time, labour and fuel, and also cut down on wastage during the fishing season. Moreover, it prevented the smoke from getting into the eyes of the women, for the trays directed the smoke upwards into the sky and made it generally possible to keep the surroundings cleaner and more orderly.

The office of the United Nations Children's Education Fund (UNICEF) in Ghana, with which the NCWD had been working very closely in educating women on child-care and nutrition, decided to assist the NCWD in promoting the use of the Chorkor oven in many more villages. In 1983, UNICEF imported a large quantity of wire mesh for the purpose, because the local factory could not keep up with the demand for the mesh. A staff member of the Food Research Institute taught carpenters in the villages how to make the trays, and within a short time women in nearby villages, who had seen how effective the new ovens were, were coming to the NCWD offices with requests for assistance in obtaining wire mesh, for there were masons and carpenters who could build the ovens for them. This particular project, which involved the use of relatively inexpensive and unsophisticated technology, shows that new improved technology is more likely to be readily accepted if it is based on the same principles as those traditionally used by the people for whom the technology is designed, and if the people are consulted about the design at every stage. This is what the Food Research Institute in Ghana had done. On account of this, the benefits to be derived from this new technology were obvious to the women, and they were prepared to invest money in the construction of the ovens. The NCWD organized workshops, as it had done with all the income-generating projects, to educate the women on how to manage their fish-smoking business.

This project did not suffer from the organizational and management problems of other income-generating activities, for the women did not have to come together as a co-operative with a common fund to be able to run a common facility, like the gari-making or oil-extraction machinery. They continued their fish smoking on an individual basis. The close association into which they were organized in their villages served mainly as a useful link with sources for the supply of wire mesh, for as a group, they could buy the mesh in bulk at a much cheaper price. The NCWD also used these associations for its educational programmes.

One thing that comes out clearly from these activities with rural women is that in order to achieve the desired

78

results with educational and other programmes for women, the particular group of women must be convinced that you have their welfare at heart. Once you have demonstrated that you can help them improve upon their standard of living, and they are convinced that you are genuinely interested in their welfare, they lose their suspicion of educated city women. From then on, they are prepared to listen to and try to appreciate the arguments about the need to allow their daughters to complete school and have some training before they get married, and the need to limit the size of their family as well as space births for their own sake and for the sake of their children.

Like the other income-generating projects, the fish-smoking project increased the income-earning capacity of the women, making it possible for them to supplement the family income. This meant that they now could pay for better medical services, and in some cases, vocational or higher education for their children and other dependants. Moreover, the increased availability of fish meant more protein in the family diet and, therefore, better nutrition.

The project can also have far-reaching national significance. It has not been possible to assess its full impact on the supply of fish throughout the country, or on the use of fuel-wood, but it is clear that in those villages where the Chorkor ovens are extensively used, the fishermen no longer have to throw fish back into the sea when there is a bumper catch. And it is this fact that has made the men in the fishing villages along the coast take an active interest in helping their women to build more of the ovens. It has already been pointed out that the women control the money they earn. With increased income comes greater self-confidence and higher self-esteem. Some of them started saving with the banks, and they have been able to obtain loans to buy canoes and/or fishing nets, thus increasing their access to more fish for processing. An expansion in the fish-smoking activity means that they can now provide employment for members of their extended family as well as other members of the community, something which brings them added respect and status in their own family and in their community. When one such successful fish-monger was asked how her husband felt about her success, she said proudly, 'Ah, he now calls me "Missus"'. In Ghanaian society, only women married under Ordinance law, Christian marriage, and in some cases, under Moslem law, especially when the marriage is monogamous, use the husband's name, and are called "Mrs. so-and-so'. It is generally understood that such women are not as sub-ordinate to their husbands as those married under Customary law, for they have more security and more say within the marriage than Customary law wives, since they cannot normally be divorced until after lengthy legal divorce procedures. The woman who made this remark was non-literate, and was the second of three wives married under Customary law. She knew her marital status was not going to change simply because she was making more money than her co-wives, but she understood her husband's new attitude to mean that he had tacitly given her an elevated status in their relationship. He no longer con-sidered her to be subordinate to him. She was an equal, and his calling her 'Missus' rather than by her name is a sign of respect, a reflection of the woman's new status in the community in which she lives. It is quite clear that if such a woman decides that she wants to limit the number of children that she wants to have, or expresses an opinion on how her children should be educated, the husband will listen to her and take her views into consideration. In the unending search for effective ways of improving the status of women in society, such women have become effective role-models for the women in their communities.

Handicrafts

As has been discussed above, the major economic activities of the majority of women living in the rural areas are farming, food-processing and fish-curing. Because these activities are seasonal, many of the women take up various types of handicrafts during the off-season, using materials that are readily available in the locality. The major activities are pottery, basket-weaving, mat-weaving, spinning and bead-making. Women potters in various parts of the country were assisted with small loans and technical advice to upgrade the traditional methods of production. With the help of the Technology Consultancy Centre of the University of Science and Technology, a Technical officer of the NCWD was able to design a more efficient spinning wheel for the women of the Northern Region Women engaged in basket-weaving and mat-weaving also benifitted from the small loans scheme of the NCWD. A bead-making group at Daabaa has been selected for special mention here because of the impact their activity had on the young women in the village.

The ornamental use of beads is very popular with women of all ethnic groups in Ghana. Some men, especially chiefs and fetish priests, also wear beads on special occasions, and bead-making has been, for years, a traditional craft of both men and women in the country.

Daabaa is a village in the Ashanti Region. Farming is the major economic activity in the village, but the men also make beads which the women buy and sell to market women in Kumasi. There is a brisk trade in beads in the Kumasi central market where traders come from different parts of the country and also from Côte d'Ivoire to buy beads in large quantities to retail.

The NCWD Regional Secretary in Kumasi heard about the bead-making activity in Daabaa and paid a visit to the village. She realized that the bead-making was a men's activity in Daabaa. She knew, however, that women were making beads in other parts of the country, and she decided to encourage the women to take up bead-making. The major problem was to persuade the men to agree to give up their monopoly and teach the women how to make beads.

In discussions with the men, the NCWD Regional Secretary learnt that their major problem was with getting an adequate supply of dyes of different colours. The Technology Consultancy Centre at the University of Science and Technology was already assisting some bead-making groups with dyes, so the NCWD Regional Secretary promised the men that she would try and arrange a supply of dyes for them. After the initial supply of dyes, she was able to persuade the men to agree to teach some of the women how to make beads. The men agreed. Her next problem was how to persuade enough women to agree to learn bead-making. The activity had been in the hands of men for so long that many of the women, especially the older ones, had assumed that it was a male activity and that there was a taboo about women making beads. Fortunately, there were younger women who were prepared to venture into this new activity, so a small bead-making group of women was organized in Daabaa. The young women learnt the bead-making technology in no time, and they revolutionalized the whole activity by introducing new shapes and colour combinations in the beads they made. The men had, up till that time, made beads of shapes, sizes and colours that had acquired some cultural significance over the years.

Like all the other income-generating activities, the bead-making project effectively increased the income- earning capacity of the women, thereby improving their self-esteem and enabling them take better care of their families. But the project did more than that. The liberating effect that it had on the women was, to some extent, comparable to that of the Essam oil-extraction project. Here were women successfully taking up an activity that had hitherto been dominated by men, and in the process breaking new ground in bead-making designs. They now knew that there was no difference in the basic intelligence of men and women, and that as long as an activity did not require excessive physical energy, there was nothing that a woman could not do if she only put her mind to it.

In the search for effective ways of improving the status of women in society, the experience in Ghana has shown that income-generating programmes are important as the focus for mobilising women for programmes that are designed to create in them confidence in their own capabilities, so that they could participate effectively in, and contribute to the development of their communities. The liberating effect that these projects have is more permanent and more far-reaching than any lectures on the equality of the sexes.

Chapter 3

THE WAY FORWARD

In the preceding chapters, we have been looking at the impact that the United Nations Decade for Women had on the emancipation of women in Africa. At the end of the Decade in 1985, many were those who were justifiably disappointed at how little progress had been made in realizing the objectives of the Decade. Some were worried that the end of the Decade would mean an end to the focus on women's issues, and therefore an end to the commitment on the part of individual governments and international agencies to work towards the realization of total emancipation of women in all societies.

The optimists felt differently. They agreed that the achievements of the Decade had, in some areas, fallen far short of the great expectations that the period had held for many. They knew that the brainwashing effect that constant repetition of religious, cultural and other justification for a woman's subordinate position and a man's superiority was too far-reaching and too deeply rooted in the subconscious of many men and women for there to have been a dramatic change in attitudes over a ten-year period. They were, however, fully conscious of the significant achievements which held promise for the future. The Decade had succeeded in creating among men and women throughout the world a keen awareness of the plight of women, and, what is more important, a willingness to do something about it. Moreover, major obstacles to the emancipation of women had now been identified, and so had the procedures for removing such obstacles. They felt that the process that International Women's Year set in motion in 1975 had gathered such momentum during the

Decade, that it cannot be stopped until the objectives of the Decade are fully realized in all countries.

In Africa, those working with and for women have been encouraged by the fact that men, some of whom had initially been very cynical about the objectives of the Decade, now understand and appreciate the impact that the emancipation of women can have on the level of consciousness of the society as a whole, and on the development of their individual countries. Men are the policy- and decision-makers in these countries, and the change in their attitudes has significant implications for the women's cause. The support that individual African governments gave to the United Nations Conferences held in 1975 (Mexico), 1980 (Copenhagen) and 1985 (Nairobi), as well as the preparatory meetings leading to them, was very encouraging. In particular, the hosting of the end-of-Decade Conference in Nairobi, was a clear indication of the commitment of African governments to work for the emancipation of their women, and every effort has to be made to sustain that commitment.

The impact of the Decade on African women has not been less noticeable. The creation, in many countries, of national machineries such as women's bureaux and women's councils, gave national significance to women's issues, which, up to that time, had mainly been the concern of individual voluntary women's organizations. The strengthening of the women's units of various government departments and ministries, and the funding by international agencies of projects and programmes for women meant that women were now receiving a lot more attention than previously. Rural women, in particular, who had been neglected for years, suddenly found themselves at the centre of attention. The salutary effect that this had on their own self-esteem was a necessary first step to the consciousness-raising and awareness-creation that the Decade brought.

The complexity of the issue of women's emancipation is very well reflected in the documents adopted at the three

United Nations Conferences - "The World Plan of Action" adopted in Mexico in 1975, "The Programme of Action for the Second Half of the United Nations Decade for Women" adopted in Copenhagen in 1980, and the "Forward-looking Strategies for the Advancement of Women Beyond the UN Decade for Women to the Year 2000" adopted in Nairobi in 1985. These documents spell out in great detail the programmes and activities that need to be implemented, at the level of individual countries and globally, in order to ensure that women the world over achieve full equality with men in all aspects.

What follows in this section is an attempt to highlight some of the ways in which national machineries and NGOs (Non-governmental Organisations), on the one hand, and international agencies on the other can effectively work for the emancipation of women on the continent.

National Machineries and Non-governmental Organizations

When the United Nations declared 1975 as International Women's Year, it also enjoined member-states to set up national machineries which would, among other things, study the condition of women, initiate programmes to promote the emancipation of women, and monitor progress made in this direction. Up to that time, matters relating to the status of women and other women's issues had not properly been on the agenda of governments. They had, from time to time, been brought up by concerned voluntary women's organizations, who, in some cases, had had to resort to protest demonstrations in order to draw national attention to a particular source of injustice to women. National machineries with staff paid by government would provide full-time staff whose sole responsibility would be to deal with all aspects of women's concerns and their status in individual countries. The establishment of the national machineries would also ensure that there is a permanent channel of communication between women and the government, so that most pressing issues affecting women can be routinely dealt with without recourse to protest demonstrations or formal presentation of petitions by women's organizations.

The form that the national machineries have taken in Africa varies from country to country. However, the following major types may be identified. In Zimbabwe, there is a Ministry for Women and Youth headed by a cabinet minister, and in some Francophone countries such as Côte d'Ivoire and the Federal Republic of Cameroon, there are Ministries for Women's Affairs; in Kenya, Sierra Leone and Swaziland the national machinery is located in the Department of Social Welfare, and works to an advisory board. In the Gambia and Ghana, the national machinery is a statutory body headed by an Executive Secretary who is responsible to a policy-making board. In some other countries, the women's wing of the ruling political party functions as the official machinery that deals with women's issues.

Each of these various models of national machineries has its advantages and disadvantages. In a country such as Zimbabwe, the fact that there is a cabinet minister responsible for women's issues means that there is somebody at the highest decision-making level who can bring such issues to the attention of government. However, voluntary women's organizations may have difficulty working with such a highly-placed government official, especially if there are differences of opinion about certain government policies and how they affect women. In the Kenya, Sierra Leone and Swaziland model, care has to be taken to expand the programmes of the Women's Bureaux to include broader issues such as legislation as well as traditions that affect the status of women, otherwise the programmes of the Bureaux would not be very different from what are traditionally dealt with by the women's unit of the Department of Social Welfare and Community Development. The Gambia and Ghana model is independent of any government department. However, the fact that it is directly under the office of the Head of State means that sometimes pressing issues may have to wait until the Head of State can give audience to the board, or the board may have to channel its requests or recommendations through a cabinet minister whose presentation of the issues may not be as convincing as the board would have wished.

One point is clear, however, that the creation of the women's bureaux and councils in various African countries has meant a focus on women's issues at the national level to a degree not known in any of these countries before 1975. The creation of these offices has also meant access to funding for specifically women-related activities. Up to that time, when funding was provided to individual government departments such as Agriculture, Education or Community Development, it was not always possible to ensure that an adequate proportion of that funding was used to promote activities for women. Such offices also have a responsibility for co-ordinating the activities of government departments and voluntary organizations in so far as they affect women. In some countries, this has made it possible to achieve, to some extent, an integrated approach to dealing with the various problems affecting women. It is essential that, from time to time, an evaluation is made of the activities of such national machineries so that they can be strengthened, where necessary, and enabled to be an effective instrument for the promotion of the emancipation of women.

Voluntary women's organizations in Africa range from those of particular religious bodies through market women's organizations and professional women's organizations to the ladies' clubs of individual departments, corporations and other establishments. They are, in general, charitable organizations that raise funds to provide a service for underprivileged groups in the society - orphans, the handicapped, the sick, rural communities and so on. A few of them, such as the professional women's groups also organize, from time to time, seminars and

88

workshops to educate women on certain issues that are of importance to them, such as laws affecting women, managing a small business, careers available to women and where to train for these, problems of working women and so on. In recent years, the Association of Business and Professional Women which has branches in various African countries, has been establishing pilot income-generating projects with some women's groups, and using the projects to train women in business management.

One noticeable result of the consciousness-raising that came with the United Nations Decade for Women was the formation of ladies' clubs in a number of work-places. The main objectives of such groups were to work to improve the image of the female worker, to provide moral and, where necessary, material support for their members, and to monitor and take action on cases of discrimination against their members, such as cases of sexual harassment or discrimination in promotion.

In many countries, individual voluntary women's organizations work on their own, and very little effort is made to relate their activities to those of other organizations. For example, church women's groups of individual denominations would operate their own programmes, and perhaps once or twice in a year organize a programme across denominations under the auspices of the Christian Council of the particular country. Ladies' clubs in various work-places may once in a while organize a joint programme under the auspices of the Trade Union movement or a similar organization in the country, and so on. In a few cases, there are umbrella organizations such as the Ghana Assembly of Women, and the Lutsango Lakangwane of Swaziland whose membership include a number of Non-governmental Organizations (NGOs), but these organizations are by no means all-inclusive, except, perhaps, the Sierra Leone Women's Association for National Development (WAND), the NGO umbrella organization that was inaugurated in 1988.

NGOs in Africa have been very effective in sensitizing

women on various issues that affect them. They have been able to create a feeling of solidarity among women, and have in many cases provided support, such as the free legal aid for underprivileged women provided by the Ghana branch of the International Federation of Women Lawyers (FIDA). The energies of these organizations in individual countries could be better harnessed if they were united under a national federation or council of women's organizations. It would then be possible for such a body to raise enough funds from all the different women's organizations to acquire permanent offices with a few full-time staff assisted by volunteers. With such a structure, the national umbrella NGO could, for example, provide necessary guidance to its members, especially new organizations, on what programmes they could usefully embark on. It would also be in a better position to publicize and give national significance to major annual programmes and activities of its member organizations. Moreover, it would be able to co-ordinate the activities of its members so that there is minimum overlapping of programmes, thereby giving better focus to the activities, and ensuring effective use of available resources by directing their utilization in the areas that need priority attention. Such a body would also be a valuable link between the government national machinery and NGOs, and the two could work in close collaboration for the best results. The major functions of the women's bureaux would be to co-ordinate women-related activities of government departments and conduct major research. They can then use the information gathered as the basis for advising government on what measures need to be taken to deal with the problems identified. The bureaux should also be a central point where research materials and other information on women in the given country can be obtained. They will also be in a position to provide all NGOs, through the national NGO body, information on its research findings and material from international organizations working on women's issues in other parts of the world, so that such information can filter through to women at all levels of society. This will help broaden the outlook of local NGOs and provide them with new ideas for worthwhile programmes and activities. The national machineries can also learn from the NGOs, for many of them have been dealing with one aspect or other of issues affecting women for many years, and the experience they have gained should be of immense value to officers of the national machineries. The two bodies can jointly organize leadership training for individual NGOs in order to strengthen their organizational capabilities. They will also be in a position to help individual women's groups identify sources of financial support for their projects and activities.

Co-operation between the natioanl machinery and the umbrella NGO body can only bring immense benefits to women. Unfortunately, the level of co-operation between national machineries and NGOs in many countries in Africa has not been as high as it should be because the functions of the national machineries have, in many cases, not been clearly defined or understood. The women's bureaux have been seen as an unequal rival organization trying to do on a bigger scale what individual NGOs have been doing for years; much the same way as proprietors of small businesses would look on a big multinational company that starts operating in the same kind of business. Since national machineries and women's voluntary orgnizations are all working for the same goal, namely the improvement of the condition of women in their societies, every effort should be made by the national machineries to allay the fears of the NGOs. One way of achieving this is for the national machinery not to compete with NGOs in raising funds from the same local sources. The national machineries can also assist well-organized NGOs by guaranteeing them for projects that are funded from external sources. In Africa, most NGOs do not have offices with paid staff. The office of the organization is usually located in the house of whoever happens to be the secretary at any given time. This makes it difficult for foreign agencies to fund major projects by NGOs in Africa. In Ghana, the NCWD was able to assist in some cases where foreign NGOs, which normally would fund projects by local NGOs and not government agencies, needed assurances about the ability of a local NGO to implement a particular project.

In the struggle to improve the quality of life of, especially, the disadvantaged women in Africa, a division in the women's front is a luxury that we cannot afford. It is essential, therefore, that all concerned women, especially educated women, should work closely together to achieve a marked improvement in the condition of women in the shortest possible time, whether they work with a national machinery or with an NGO.

International Agencies

Much of the funding for women's projects and programmes has come, and still continues to come from the Specialised Agencies of the United Nations, in particular, and from agencies and governments of individual countries, especially in the industrialized world. Four major areas to which such funding has been directed are research, income-generating projects, training and study tours.

Research

The value of research, as a means of identifying what the issues are, as well as providing the necessary information on which programmes for dealing with those issues can be based, has already been pointed out. Much of the research done during the Decade into various aspects of women's life and their condition in individual countries was funded by international agencies, and the documentation that resulted from such research has been valuable indeed. Sometimes, funding was also provided for conferences and seminars at which the major research findings were discussed, making it possible for publicity to be given to such findings, and thereby making the general public aware of vital issues affecting women in their society. In Ghana, for example, USAID funded extensive research into various aspects of the condition of women, and also funded a one-week conference at which the research findings were discussed. Women from other English-speaking West African countries were sponsored to attend this conference, and their contribution was valuable in indicating some of the ways in which certain specific women's issues were being tackled in their particular countries. In Swaziland, the International Planned Parenthood Federation funded research into laws affecting women, and the information on specific individual issues was published in very simple language in small booklets so as to make them accessible to as many women as possible.

Some of the research was also linked to the income-generating projects. They studied the procedures used by the women, their status in their community and other related matters before the implementation of the project, and the impact of the project on the women, economically and socially, after its implementation. Where new technology was successfully introduced, these were described in detail, with illustrative diagrams, and published, so that it can be duplicated in other countries where women are engaged in similar activities. In Ghana, this was done with the income-generating activities undertaken under the Netherlands/ILO Technologies for Rural Women project. UNICEF also published English and French versions of a booklet describing the Chorkor fish-smoking oven and explaining how it works, thus making the information available to women in both English-speaking and French-speaking countries. UNICEF had earlier funded a one-week seminar in Accra for women from Guinea, Benin and Togo to expose them to this new fish-smoking technology so that they could introduce it in their own countries. UNICEF also made it possible for the Chorkor oven to be included in the appropriate technologies that were exhibited and/or demonstrated at the End-of-Decade Conference in Nairobi, Kenya, in 1985.

There is no doubt that much of the consciousness-raising and awareness-creation that was achieved during the Decade about women's issues was as a result of the extensive research work that was done. The evidence provided by the facts and figures of the research findings was too convincing for men and women as well as governments to ignore, and in many cases steps were taken to do something about the particular situation which had been identified as being detrimental to women. Not surprisingly, response to such research findings has been slowest where they are related to aspects of the culture and traditions of the society, such as those discussed in Chapter 1. However, the fact that these matters are now being discussed in the open is a healthy sign, and as long as the discussion and the education on the need for change continue, there is every hope that in due course the necessary change in attitude will take place for these traditional practices to be either modified, where necessary, or ultimately eradicated. One can only hope that although the Decade is over, international agencies will continue to fund valuable research into issues affecting women.

A point that needs to be made, however, is that although many women in Africa were happy about their being the centre of attention, they soon become tired of being asked numerous questions, some seen by them to be too personal or improper, especially when the benefits to them of such questioning were not apparent or clearly articulated to them. In Ghana, the NCWD realized that in order to have the full co-operation of the women, research projects that involved long periods of observation of the way women went about various activities, or involved lengthy interviews should, as far as possible, be followed with a project that is of obvious material benefit to the women or to the community. Such projects could be the provision of good drinking water for a village in the form of a well; the supply of some basic educational material such as home science equipment for the village school, or the provision of some simple technology to relieve the women of the drudgery involved in some activity that they were engaged in. In other words, while research is valuable for identifying the factors, positive or negative, that affect the lives of women, what the village woman is interested in is to see an improvement in the condition in which she lives. She cannot be expected to appreciate the value to her of the documentation of her particular problems, if there is no indication of possible relief in the foreseeable future. If local agencies working with and for women are to be effective, their activities must be seen to bring some change for the better for the women who are the subject of research. This is particularly important if the women's level of education is not high enough for them to appreciate the value of research. In the absence of this, local people working with women may soon find that they cannot sustain the interest and the co-operation of the women they work with. It is important that donor agencies help local people to be effective, by making provision for the necessary follow-up action to major research that is undertaken.

Income-generating Activities

Funding from external sources for income-generating activities for women is vital, especially where new technology is to be introduced. This is because the cost of the equipment needed is usually much too high for the women. Moreover, their suspicion of new machinery that they do not understand, and the risk of such machinery breaking down and creating problems for them, make them hesitant about investing the large sums of money involved, even when the benefits may be reasonably clear to them. It was shown in Chapter 2 that the women farmers and those engaged in fish-smoking were prepared to fund the projects with their savings or with bank loans because the investment required was not too heavy, and the equipment not completely new to them.

It is this fact that makes external funding for projects still necessary. Another reason is that with the fluctuations in the value of the currencies of many African countries, capital that may be borrowed from a bank may fall far short of the price of the equipment by the time it is imported or manufactured, and the women's group may find themselves saddled with a huge debt that may very well break them. Funding from external sources for projects is, therefore, very vital if a reasonable level of progress is to be maintained in the area of income-generating activities for women.

It is, however, necessary to draw attention to some factors that may have the effect of reducing the benefits of some of these projects. For example, it was pointed out under the Mafi-Kumasi project that one of the reasons why the project was not as successful as expected was the fact that the factory was completely free. The women did not make any contribution towards the construction of the building or the purchase of the equipment. The result was that they did not have the level of commitment that was needed for the success of the project. People tend to put a higher value on things they work for, or at least have contributed to, than they do on things that are given absolutely free. Of course, there are cases, such as projects for people in refugee camps, where free gifts may be absolutely necessary. In the Mafi-Kumasi case, however, the women were in a position to make some financial contribution to the project. Where such contribution from the women is possible, funding agencies need to work closely with the local people responsible for implementing the project to identify the type and level of contribution, in cash or in kind, that beneficiaries of a project can make, so as to ensure their commitment to it.

From time to time, funding agencies change the type of project they are prepared to support, and groups or countries who need such funding have to tailor their projects accordingly. For example, it was believed, some time ago, that one way of ensuring that women had fewer children was to encourage them to work outside the home so that the pressure of inadequate child-care facilities would force them to have longer periods between the birth of one child and the next, and also to have fewer children. It was for this reason that a family-planning organization funded, in 1977, the renovation of a basket-weaving training centre that was located about three kilometres from the nearest village in the Volta Region of Ghana. Those women who trained there soon decided that it was more convenient for them to do the basket-weaving at home than to travel the distance every day to the centre, even though that meant their losing access to large quantities of the raw materials they needed and at a cheaper price. The project never took off the way it was intended, although the centre became a useful place for holding one-day seminars on various topics with women from nearby villages, and also for organizing one-week residential basket-weaving training programmes.

Another example relates to the belief of many donor agencies that co-operative societies are the solution to the problem of the small producer. Co-operatives may have been very successful in many countries, but in Ghana, the experience has been that many of the small producers have operated reasonably successfully on their own, or with members of their family for so long that they have difficulty in giving up their independence in order to be part of a co-operative society. It was pointed out in Chapter 2 that problems that the Mafi-Kumasi Gari-processing Co-operative faced made the NCWD no longer insist that the women's groups it worked with register as co-operative societies.

The NCWD later initiated a study into the different *susu* systems, operated by market women, to see if they can be used as a basis for devising a modified co-operative system that would be acceptable to the women. The susu system is a means of raising necessary capital, interest-free, for members of a group. In the traditional susu system each member of the group contributes a certain pre-determined sum of money every week or every month as the case may be. This amount is given to one member of the group at a time, so that over a period of weeks or months, each member would have got a fairly large sum of money as capital to expand her trade or to spend on some other urgent business. For the small-scale trader, this is an effective means of saving money, especially since she does not have to interrupt her work to go to the bank, during banking hours, with relatively small amounts of money. The point being made here is that since local conditions differ from country to country, and may even be different in parts of the same country, it is important that before methods that may have been successful in other communities are tried out in new situations, the conditions in the new situation should be fully understood, and if necessary, the new method adapted to suit that new situation.

Attention has been drawn to these aspects of international funding because it is frustrating to invest good money in a project and not achieve the desired results. Many local organizations, including government departments, usually do not have enough funds from local sources to implement their programmes, and there is, therefore, the danger of their accepting any offer of funding that comes, without initially examining clearly the full implications of the different aspects of the project, including the use of foreign experts. Care should always be taken to ensure that, as far as possible, the final project document reflects both the objectives of the funding agency and the particular needs of the proposed beneficiaries. This means that the local agencies must themselves be fully conversant with, and sensitive to the felt needs of the people for whom a project is designed.

Training and Study Tours

Staff-training in research, administration, management of projects as well as in various aspects of women's work has been, and continues to be one vital way in which international agencies provide valuable assistance to developing countries. Given the economic straits in which many African countries find themselves, such assistance will continue to be needed for some time to come, especially where the training needed is not available in the particular country, and scarce hard currency has to be spent on sending individuals to other countries for training. The experience in Ghana during the Decade showed that where such training was in the management of projects or in the organization of women's groups, training in another African country, or in another Third World country, such as India, was of immense value. This is because the trainees could relate to the situation in those countries, and could see similarities in the projects and in the condition of women there, so that the relevance of the training was very clear to them, and they could readily apply what they had learnt to the groups they work with in their communities.

Some of the training programmes sponsored during the Decade were for groups of women engaged in one or the other economic activity. For example, groups of women from Eastern and Southern Africa were sponsored on trips to West Africa to train in some specific income-generating activities. These training programmes were also intended to give the women exposure to the operations of women entrepreneurs, for the economic activities of women from that part of Africa tend to be on a small scale. Such training programmes were rather expensive, for it would have been cheaper for one woman entrepreneur to be sent to train groups of women in those countries. However, the exposure of these women to how individual women run fairly large businesses in manufacturing, food-processing and trade had an impact that no number of lectures and workshops on how to operate a big business could have made possible. In most cases, there were follow-up visits by one of the women entrepreneurs to the trainees in their countries to see how they were putting what they had learnt into practice, and to help them solve the initial problems in setting up their businesses.

In addition to exposing such groups of women to new areas of economic activity, the impact that such programmes had on the individual women's perception of themselves and their capabilities was very noticeable. When Ghanaian women from the rural areas who went on similar training programmes in Kenya came back, it was clear that the trip had given them self-confidence and a determination to work for a more effective organization of the particular women's group they belonged to. They probably could have had the same training in Ghana, but the exposure to a different environment and the confidence that comes with successfully adapting to a different culture, had a noticeable liberating effect on them, and they are performing very effective leadership roles in their communities. These programmes also fostered a feeling of solidarity among women from different parts of the continent.

The African Training and Research Centre for Women of the United Nations Economic Commission for Africa, based in Addis Ababa, played a leading role in facilitating such group travel and training. It had five regional centres, located in different parts of the continent, which co-ordinated such group travel. One can only hope that international agencies such as the specialized agencies of the United Nations, agencies and governments of individual countries, the Commonwealth Secretariat, religious organizations such as the World Council of Churches and the All Africa Conference of Churches that have been supporting various programmes for women, will continue to provide such support. In the absence of such support, it will not be possible to sustain the progress made during the Decade in promoting the emancipation of women in Africa.

Conclusion

The total emancipation of women, especially in Africa, is bound to take a very long time, given the level of under-development in, particularly, the rural areas, and given the slow rate of economic growth and the level of indebtedness of many African countries, which has meant that much of national revenue is spent on servicing debts rather than on development projects. However, the Ghanaian experience, since the launching of International Women's Year, has shown how much can be achieved within a relatively short time if people in government are constantly made aware of the need to give women the opportunity to contribute effectively to national development at the highest policy-making levels; if pressure is brought on governments to enact necessary legislation that would generally improve the condition and status of women in society; if women are properly motivated; if programmes and projects for women are designed in consultation with the women concerned and are meant to meet their felt needs; and if organizers of women's programmes have the confidence of the women they work with.

It is said that a journey of a thousand miles begins with the first step. For many rural African women, the United Nations Decade for Women gave them the opportunity to take a first giant step on the long road to emancipation. The Decade succeeded in creating in them a keen awareness of the unfair subordinate position that society has imposed on women, and in motivating them to do something about it. What is now needed to maintain the momentum is a sustained and concerted effort on the part of governmental and non-governmental organizations, both local and international, to initiate and implement for women, educational and development programmes that take due cognizance of the cultural values and the particular needs of each society. Above all, women, especially educated, privileged women, must take active part in programmes for the less fortunate women in their communities in order to help them increase

their pace and catch up with them, for there is an urgent
need for all of us to ensure that we reach the end of the long
journey to emancipation in the not-too-distant future.

REFERENCES

Danquah, S.A. 1978. Some aspects of mental health of Ghanaian women: Female psychoneuroses and social problems. In *Proceedings of the Seminar on Ghanaian Women in Development.*. (Mimeo.). Accra: NCWD Library.

Ghana Government 1985. *PNDC Law 111, Law on Intestate Succession.*

International Labour Organization 1985. *Technologies for Rural Women - Ghana. Technical Manual No.1. Palm Oil Processing.* Adwinsa, Accra.

___ 1985. *Technologies for Rural Women - Ghana. Technical Manual No.2. Soap Manufacturing.* Adwinsa, Accra.

___ 1985. *Technologies for Rural Women - Ghana. Technical Manual No.3. Fish Smoking.* Adwinsa, Accra.

Koso-Thomas, O. 1987. *The Circumcision of Women, A Strategy for Eradication.* London: Zed Books Ltd.

Ministry of Education, Ghana. *Educational Statistics 1967/68 - 1983/84.*

National Council on Women and Development *Annual Reports* 1975-1976, 1977-1979, 1980-1984.

National Council on Women and Development 1978. *Proceedings of the Seminar on Ghanaian Women in Development.* September 1978. Vols. I & II. Accra: NCWD.

North, J. *et al.* 1975. *Ghanaian Women in Development.* (Mimeo) Accra, USAID.

Quarcoopome, A. and Ahadzie, W. 1981. *Girls' and Women's Access to Education in Rural Areas.* (unpublished) Accra: NCWD.

University of Ghana Statistics 1960/61 to 1989/90.

United Nations 1975. *World Plan of Action.*

the United Nations Decade for Women.

___   1985. Forward-Looking Strategies for the Advancement of Women Beyond the UN Decade For Women to the Year 2000.

___   1979. Convention on the Elimination of All Forms of Discrimination against Women.

UNICEF 1983. A Practical Guide to Improved Fish Smoking in West Africa. New York.

INDEX

Adidome Rural Bank, 64, 67
Adult literacy programmes, 55-56
African societies
  concept of family in, 3, 4
  female circumcision in, 34-40
  marriage in, 1-4, 6-23
  matrilineal, 7-9, 26, 27, 30
  patrilineal, 8, 9, 11, 26, 30
  widowhood rites in, 23-25
African Training and Research Centre for Women of the ECA, 99
All Africa Conference of Churches, 99
Association of Women Medical and Dental Practitioners, 46

Bortianor, 54, 55
Bride-wealth, 7-11 see also Marriage
  among the Swazi, 7-8

Children, 30, 31
  legitimacy of, 7-8
Chinese craftsmen, 59
Chorkor fish-smoking oven, 77-79, 92, 93
Commonwealth Secretariat, 99
Convention People's Party (CPP), 48

Daabaa
  bead-making at, 80-82
Damongo cassava-growing and gari-processing project, 64, 65

Divorce, 3, 19
Dowry see Bride-wealth

Essam oil-processing project, 70-75

Family planning programmes, see Fertility rate among African women
Female circumcision, 34-40
Fertility rate among African women
  factors leading to high, 30- 34
  impact of family planning programmes on, 31-32
Food Research Institute, 77, 78

Ghana Assembly of Women, 88
Ghana Education Service, 53
Ghana Food Distribution Corporation, 60
Ghana Law Reform Commission, 27
Ghana National Council on Women and Development (NCWD)
  activities of, 44-47, 69, 71, 73-78, 81, 91, 96
Ghanaian Association of University Women (GAUW), 46, 53
Ghanaian women
  carreer guidance and counselling for, 53
  education of, 49-57
  market, 43, 44
  policy-making positions by, 46-49

professional, 42, 43
   status of, 41-45

Household chores, 5-6

Illegitimacy *see* Children
Income-generating activities
   bead-making, 80-82
   farming, 61-64
   fish-smoking, 75-80
   food-processing, 65-70
   funding for, 94-97
   oil-processing, 71-75
Infant mortality, 31
Inheritance of property, 26, 27, 29,
   intestate and, 26-29
International Agencies, 91
International Federation of
   Women Lawyers (FIDA), 29,
   46, 89
International Labour Organization (ILO), 71
International Planned Parenthood Federation, 59
International Women's Year
   (1975), 45, 83-85, 100
Intestate Succession Law (1985),
   7, 27-29, 45 *see also*
   Inheritance of property

Koso-Thomas, Dr. Olayinka, 39

Legitimacy of children, *see*
   Children
Limann, President Hilla, 68
Lutsango Lakagwane (Swazi-
   land), 88

Mafi-Kumasi gari-processing
   project, 64, 66-70, 72, 74, 95,
   96

Marriage, 1-23
   bride-wealth in, 7-11
   child, 11-14
   customary law, 3, 4, 6
   monogamous, 6, 18, 20
   moslem, 3, 4, 6, 17, 21
   polygamous, 6, 14-21, 28, 29
   purdah in Islamic, 21-23
   see also Widowhood rites
Matrilineal society, 7-9, 26-28
   inheritance of property in,
   26-28
Ministries of Women's Affairs,
   86
Ministry for Women and Youth
   (Zimbabwe), 86
Ministry of Agriculture (Ghana)
   extension unit, 67, 74
   mechanization unit, 62

National machineries
   women's concerns by, 85-87
NCWD *see* Ghana National
   Council on Women and
   Development
Non-Formal Education *see* Adult
   literacy programmes
Non-Governmental Organiza-
   tions (NGOs), 53, 85, 88-91

Oduro, Mr. J.D., 70, 71, 74, 75

Patrilineal society, 7, 8, 26
Polygamy, 14-21, 26, 36
Purdah, 21-23

Research into women's life and
   their condition, 91-94

Sierra Leone Women's Association for National Develop-

ment (WAND), 88
Soap-making, 70, 71, 73
Somanya, 54, 55
Specialized Agencies of the
United Nations, 99

Technologies for Rural Women,
71, 92
Netherlands government's
contributions to, 71, 72
Technology Consultancy Centre
(TCC), 72, 81
Training programmes for
women, 98, 99

UNICEF, 77, 78, 92
United Nations Convention on
the Elimination of All Forms
of Discrimination Against
Women, 13

United Nations Decade for
Women, 28, 44, 45, 53, 83, 84
impact on Africa of, 84, 88,
100
United States Agency for
International Development
(USAID), 59, 66-68, 92

Vocational and professional
training for female school-
leavers, 54
Voluntary Women's Organizations, 87, 88

Women's bureaux and councils,
86, 87
Women Lawyers' Association
in Ghana see International
Federation of Women
Lawyers (FIDA)